"Larry Correia tells the simple truth in *In Defense of the Second Amendment*: 'Nothing stops a madman with a gun, but a good guy with a gun.' It's the best explanation of why gun sales are booming as Americans realize they're on their own to stop crime as it happens. American citizens are the real first responders."
—**Jim Scoutten**, *Shooting USA*

In Defense of the Second Amendment

In Defense of the Second Amendment

IN DEFENSE
of the
SECOND AMENDMENT

Larry Correia

Foreword by Nick Searcy

Regnery Publishing
WASHINGTON, D.C.

Regnery® is a registered trademark and its colophon is a trademark of Salem Communications Holding Corporation

Cataloging-in-Publication data on file with the Library of Congress

ISBN: 978-1-68451-414-4
eISBN: 978-1-68451-415-1

Published in the United States by
Regnery Publishing,
A Division of Salem Media Group
Washington, D.C.
www.Regnery.com

Manufactured in the United States of America

10 9 8 7 6 5 4 3 2 1

Books are available in quantity for promotional or premium use. For information on discounts and terms, please visit our website: www.Regnery.com.

A well regulated Militia, being necessary to the security
of a free State, the right of the people to keep and bear Arms,
shall not be infringed.

Note to reader: Book publishing takes time, and since this went to press, the U.S. Bureau of Alcohol, Tobacco, Firearms, and Explosives has likely changed its regulations because, well, as an organization it is malicious, capricious, malignantly dysfunctional, and generally sucks. Make sure you check the current rules.

Foreword by Nick Searcy

Before I met Larry Correia, bestselling author, I met Larry Correia, vicious, bloodthirsty serial Twitter murderer.

I didn't know who Larry was when I first befriended him on social media. I just knew he tore up silly leftist dumbasses on the internet the way Michael Moore tore up extra-large supreme meatza pizzas. And Larry did so hilariously, with biting sarcasm, incisive wit, and invincible logic. I immediately saw him as an irreplaceable ally in the never-ending Twitter War, and I felt a kinship, as both of us do not play with leftist idiots well. We both had waded into the social media sewer with all our guns blazing, laughing hysterically as we slaughtered stupid Democrat-worshipping brainwashed losers day after day, laughing all the way.

It was only later that I realized that Larry was also a great and prolific fiction writer, with an output as long as my acting resume, and that Larry was exactly the rare kind of conservative I had been saying for years that we needed—the conservative who created art, the conservative who entered the world of storytelling, a world that for too long had been ceded to zombified leftists like Stephen King, Don Winslow, and other once-talented writers whose works had become predictable groaners because of their seemingly irresistible need to infuse them with trite, unrealistic, virtue-signaling leftist ideology.

As a fellow warrior in a creative field myself, the world of cinematic storytelling, I felt I had found a brother.

In reading Larry's Monster Hunter novels, you realize that underpinning all the exciting action, banter, and bloodshed there is a strong, sensible moral code—a code that goes beyond mere legality and enters the realm of right and wrong. Often the hero in a Correia work steps *outside* of the framework of the law—which, if followed to the letter, would have allowed evil to triumph—and makes a moral choice that might technically be illegal.

At the same time that I was reading Larry's books, I was involved in a television show called *Justified* that featured a main character, Raylan Givens, who also frequently stepped outside of what the law dictated he should do and did what his conscience told him was the right thing to do. And, since I played Raylan's boss, I was the one who ultimately had to decide when I would let Raylan break the law to do the right thing and when I would bust him because he had gone too far.

You see, the law itself is not capable of stopping evil from happening. It is only there to punish the perpetrator after the crime has gone down—which means that the victims are already dead, or raped, or had their life and property destroyed, et cetera, and it is too late to save them.

Which is why the Second Amendment is the only thing that makes Americans capable of preventing pure evil from victimizing them. A law will not and cannot do it.

There are laws against murder. Murders still happen. Same with rape, armed robbery, breaking and entering, car theft, and on and on. The only thing a law can do is punish a criminal after an innocent has been victimized—and in Democrat-run cities with no-cash bail and corrupt prosecutors, the law won't even do that.

The Democrats—and some leftist Republicans—who are pushing all these gun laws know this. They know that all the gun laws they can dream up will apply only to people who obey them. Criminals, by definition, will not obey laws. So why are they doing it when they know it won't stop criminals?

This may come as a shock to you—and it may not—but the anti-gun people are not concerned about criminals. They really don't care what the lawbreakers do, and when you see them drooling over every mass shooting before the bodies are even identified as just another opportunity to advance their agenda, they prove that. Their hysterical gun laws are targeted, with a laser focus, *only* at law-abiding gun owners. The red dots from the infrared sights on the anti-gunners' figurative AR-15s (which they stupidly still think stands for Assault Rifle-15) will never be on the chests of the mass shooters, or the serial killers, or the armed robbers or rapists or pedophiles, but solely on their true prey: the legal American gun owners who believe in the right to self-defense, the right to bear arms, and the right to protect their families, their properties, and themselves with force.

Because the ultimate goal of the Left is to outlaw self-defense.

They want you unable to defend your life with deadly force, even when a criminal is coming for your life with deadly force. Why? Because then they know you will be totally dependent, for your safety, for your health care, for your food, for every single thing that makes you able to exist, on the totalitarian government that they intend to install.

Think I'm exaggerating? Leftists have done this all over the world, in North Korea, in Cuba, in Venezuela, in the USSR, and now even in Australia, England, and Canada. And they will do it here if we let them.

Larry Correia understands this, and he imbues his fiction with this powerful idea, and that is why it has resonated with so many throughout the world—because, unlike leftist fiction, *it makes sense.*

And now he has turned his sights on a nonfictional defense of the Second Amendment. I want the whole world to read it. Like Larry's fiction, this book will knock you on your ass, make you laugh, and steel your resolve to *never* let the good, law-abiding people of this nation become disarmed and helpless in the face of government tyranny.

I am proud to stand with Larry Correia in defending the Second Amendment, and when you read this book, you will be too.

Bring it on.

—Nick Searcy
July 23, 2022

Chapter One

Guns and Vultures

Every time there is a mass murder event, the vultures launch. It's fascinating in a sickening way. A bunch of people get killed, and within *minutes* the same crew of anti-gun zealots shows up all over the news and social media, pushing the same tired proposals that we've either tried before or logic tells us simply can't work. With zero hesitation they strike while the iron is hot, trying to push through legislation before there can be any coherent thought about the repercussions. We've seen this over and over and over again. We saw them succeed in England. We saw them succeed in Australia and New Zealand. We've seen it succeed here before.

Yet when anyone from my side responds to these ghouls, then we're shouted at that we're insensitive and how dare we speak about politics in this moment of tragedy. We should just shut our stupid mouths out of respect for the dead...while they are free to promote policies that will simply lead to a higher body count next time. If gun rights organizations say something, they are bloodthirsty monsters, and if they don't say anything, then their silence is damning guilt. It is hypocritical in the extreme, and when I speak out against this, I'm

1

called every name in the book, they say I want dead children in schools and malls, or they wish death upon my family. If I focus on logic or rationality, I'm a cold-hearted monster. If I become angry because they are promoting policies that are flawed and will accomplish the exact opposite of their stated goals, then I am a horrible person for being angry. Perhaps I shouldn't be allowed to own guns at all.

The vultures never hesitate to lie or emotionally manipulate decent, well-meaning people who just want to keep their communities safe. They prey on the public's good intentions and lack of knowledge. If you question them, they'll browbeat you into silence. They don't want debate. They want compliance.

As soon as one of these awful events hits the news, my feed fills with "ban all guns," "damn the NRA," "hateful Christians," "Republican murderers," "evil MAGA," "white men are the real killers," or some other attack on whatever demographic is most convenient for the media to despise that week. Of course this demographic blame is assigned before anybody has a clue who the killer was.

Anytime there's another mass murder, usually in a place with strict gun control, almost always in a gun-free zone, they swoop in. During election years we've even seen the situations where the Democrat candidates have called for more gun control while the shooting was *still happening*. It's reflexive and pervasive. Details never matter. They want what they want, and they'll latch onto any tragedy as fast as possible to get it.

Most reasonable people just want to fix problems. But the vultures? They don't care. There's a crisis, they want to get something out of it. Stimulus, response. Strike while emotions are high. Some want control. Others just want to posture. The ones who are aware enough to understand that their proposals will actively make things worse are the vilest kind of scum.

Every member of the gun culture watches as these events unfold and thinks, *Hell, here we go again.* It is sad, but when these things happen, my people are following the news, and before we can even begin to process what's happening, we all end up thinking some variation of *Please don't let the bad guy be someone the news can somehow make out to be like me...* Even though the vast majority of the time the shooter isn't one of us, has nothing to do with us, and (in reality) people like us are the last line of defense against them, it doesn't matter. We know we're going to get blamed.

Then they'll attack us, hound us, insult us, legislate against us, and, if they can, disarm us in more ways and places—so decent folks can be even more incapable of defending themselves the next time somebody who isn't us does something evil. Repeat. Repeat. Repeat.

Then they reveal who the shooter is.

If he is a member of any group that can possibly be tied to their political enemies, no matter how tenuously, they continue as before. If he is a delusional lunatic with no discernable political philosophy at all, they assign him to us. However, if the killer clearly aligns with *their* regular causes...

Immediately the same exact people who'd just been screeching about evil Tea Party, racist, hate-monger, right-wing, cis-hetero, whatever phantoms begin urging calm and saying not to jump to conclusions. It isn't fair to tar a big group because of the actions of a few. Watch out for that hateful rhetoric because you might inflame people.

Sure, they had no problem making sweeping generalizations and "inflaming" half the country a few minutes ago... but that's okay. Because when the vultures talk about how violent and bloodthirsty the other side is, they're just virtue signaling for their tribe. If my people were a fraction as evil and hateful as they portray us, they'd never say a word. They do it because they know it is safe to do so.

If you hear about a mass killing happening on the news, and then it suddenly vanishes the next day, with almost no national coverage, that tells you what you need to know. This is so common and ham-fisted that it has become a running joke. If an insane white racist kills ten people, we're going to have to listen to sanctimonious lectures and demands for gun control for months. If an insane black racist kills ten people, it drops off the news within twenty-four hours.

Of course the media will act all offended like this isn't the case. How dare you insinuate that their coverage is biased? But it's pain-fully, awkwardly, stupidly biased, and everyone who has paid any attention knows it.

There have been mass killings attempted by BLM supporters and Bernie Bros,[1] yet when I mention those cases to the zealots who act like this "epidemic of violence" has a single source, I'm met with clue-less stares because they haven't heard of those. In 2016 in Dallas, a psycho gunned down five cops and then got taken out *by a bomb robot*[2]—that's the kind of lurid sensationalism our sleazy media love. Yet that case got memory holed because the identity and politics of the killer weren't convenient for the narrative at the time.

Mass killers come from all races, philosophies, and walks of life. No one demographic has a monopoly on disaffected, listless, angry losers who want to make a statement. Except that's never how it is portrayed because our media and politicians have a scam to push.

We have all seen the memes and trash articles about how there is some crazy-high number of mass shootings annually. I've seen some saying that we have had over three hundred mass shootings a year, and there are political cartoons claiming there have been over 340 in the first half of this year.[3] This is a nonsense number cooked up to sell a narrative, and the only way they can get that number is by tor-turing the definition of mass shooting to any events where multiple people got shot, including things like family murder-suicides, or rival drug dealers having a gun fight. The actual number of events that fit the commonly understood definition is, as I'll show, between two and twelve in any given recent year, a tiny fraction of what the media is trying to sell.

Even then, if you stick with their ridiculous redefining of the terms, most of those three hundred "mass shootings" took place in jurisdictions with extremely strict gun control laws, like Chicago, Baltimore, and Washington, D.C.[4] By this new ridiculous standard, most mass shootings happen in cities that haven't elected a Republican in generations—yet who gets blamed for this "epidemic of violence"? The people in red states of course. Where we own piles of guns and have crime rates similar to Canada's.

I hate to break it to you, but no matter how many restrictions you put on gun ownership in Iowa, people in San Francisco are still going to get shot.

I can't accentuate enough how profoundly dishonest this behavior is. Everything the news reports is filtered through the prism of *How can I milk this for political gain?*

For example, the shooting in San Bernardino in 2015? Straight up terrorism.[5] Like dictionary-definition terrorism—violent-extremists-inspired-by-foreign-terror-organizations-preaching-about-martyrdom-style terrorism. But nope, terrorism wasn't hot right then. So the narrative became "workplace violence," which *obviously* shows a need for more gun control. If you think two coordinated, bomb-building killers just suddenly sprang into existence because of an argument at a Christmas party, you're either smoking crack or you are an avid CNN viewer.

No amount of gun control matters to a jihadist. I've talked a lot about how criminals don't care about the law. Terrorists are criminals on steroids. Militant, suicidally dedicated death cultists are in it to win it, and they aren't going away anytime soon. But hey, let's make even more places gun-free zones! That'll show them.

I'm not naïve enough to think that if some random bystander at that particular event had been armed with a concealed weapon everything would have turned out peachy. That's foolish. The only constant about gun fights is that they suck for somebody. However, a good guy with a gun *might* make a difference. The willfully ignorant will trot out their hypothetical worst-case scenarios about how an armed citizen would only make things worse, demonstrating their childlike grasp of the subject. It's difficult to make mass butchery *worse*. At best, you might end the threat. And if not—congratulations, you were at least a speed bump.

When everybody is legally disarmed, the only people who will be armed are the bad guys. Bad guys *love* that. That shooting happened in California, which has some of the strictest gun control laws in the country. Those laws ensure your only options are to run, hide, or hope. California had what is known as "may issue" CCW—a racist system where only the rich or connected are allowed to be armed—and since no movie stars or tech company CEOs were there that day, the terrorists were guaranteed their victims would be unable to shoot back (CCW stands for "carrying a concealed weapon"). California has an assault weapons ban. The terrorists didn't care. California has high-capacity-magazine bans. The terrorists didn't care. California has got all sorts of ridiculous rules with registries, approval lists, mandatory locks, safety tests, bullet buttons, and other forms of voodoo completely unintelligible to red-state America, but the terrorists still didn't care.

Of course they didn't. Because when an evil man is planning a one-way trip to commit a couple hundred felonies, including mass murder, he loves gun control laws. Gun control *protects* the bad guys. That gun-free-zone sign means they're going to get several uninterrupted minutes of carnage footage on their GoPro to stream to their propaganda websites before the cops arrive.

So what is the vultures' solution? *Make the killers mission even easier.* Further disarm the target populace. That will show them. Let's have a special report about how all of California's idiotic gun laws that utterly failed need to become mandatory in every other state. It's not like this doesn't happen all over the world—Paris, Mumbai, Beslan, and coming soon to a gun-free zone near you. There are hundreds of shootings and bombings in Africa and Asia that don't even make our news because they don't help the vulture narrative, so most Americans never even hear about them.

The media needs Americans to think that mass killings are a uniquely American experience when they clearly aren't. If they can't find a way to milk the American people for those tragedies, why bother covering them?

One thing that can always be counted on, whenever there is a mass killing by someone from a demographic that doesn't benefit the narrative, just wait a few days...and then watch for the inevitable articles about how the *real threat* in America is dangerous "right-wing extremists." If there's not a new article, an older one will suddenly become popular again. This is as reliable as clockwork. Uh-oh. There was a shooting that didn't benefit our current political goals. Quick share this link that asks, *Who are the real monsters?* Clearly the answer is always Americans who own guns. No matter what the question is, the answer is always to give the vultures more power.

Sure, a few seconds of cursory research will show that these articles about the latest looming threat are statistical bunk. Just like they conveniently redefine "terrorism," "workplace violence," "gun safety," and "mass shootings" whenever it is convenient, they cherry-pick every regular, run-of-the-mill, violent crime involving some angry white dude and label it "right-wing extremism" or "white supremacy." Of course, they could do the same thing with every violent crime involving some angry black dude and label it "black extremism," but that would be racist.

The vultures like a nice, simplistic, easily digestible narrative: *People we don't like are violent trash, so you all need to give up your rights and give us more control, and we promise this time we will protect you. Sure, we're the same government that fails constantly, but you should be helpless and count on us to be your only line of defense.*

Except reality is complicated, and there's more to violent crime than just "guns exist." Like poverty, education, drug abuse, where you live, and what violent subcultures you belong to. Crime is an extremely messy issue. Anybody who boils it all down to one root cause is trying to sell you something. In this case, they're selling gun control. Judging by how Americans purchase enough guns any given week now to arm the entire Marine Corps, apparently we aren't buying that narrative.

I've seen people freak out about recent gun sales numbers, how Americans buying guns shows "fear." Well, no kidding. Every time some evil dirtbag shoots up something, we're afraid politicians are going to ban everything. Nothing makes Americans want something like telling us we shouldn't have it, so whenever Joe Biden bloviates on the topic, gun sales go through the roof.

The vultures like their simple, repetitive formula. Everything bad is the fault of the people they don't like. You should be scared of who they want you to be scared of. Now give them more power. That's why they love racially motivated killers. Having one of those scum-bags go on a rampage is like Christmas to the vultures.

In that awful moment after the shooting starts, you don't care about the killer's motivation. It doesn't matter if he's hurting people because of their religion, politics, skin color, or because he didn't have a father figure, or the neighbor's dog told him to do it. What matters is *putting him down*. And the faster you can do that, the better.

The vultures hate when regular people fight back and prevail. They do their best to stomp on those cases. Stories of armed self-defense get squashed so thoroughly that they've convinced many low-information voters that the concept of a "good guy with a gun" is a myth. We have repeatedly seen that while the news is covering a mass casualty event, there will be other attempts within a week or two after, only the bad guy gets immediately ventilated by a bystander, and the vultures pretend it never happened. If those make the national news, it is only in passing, briefly, and then they're gone and forgotten.

The media shares part of the responsibility because they give these killers the fame they desire, but their culpability is even worse than you first think. By burying the stories where wannabe killers promptly get shot in the face by a local and die a pathetic and ignominious death, they remove the chance for shame. If all an aspiring killer goes by is what he sees on the internet, then he will believe he's going to be an unstoppable force until the cops eventually arrive in five to seventy-seven minutes. How about instead of promising them fame and importance, the media shows the ones who get gunned down by a grandma and end up as big a failure in death as they were in life?

But of course the vultures don't want aspiring killers to have second thoughts. More incidents and higher body counts get clicks and pass laws.

No matter how biased you think the press is, they're actually worse. They actively bury stories about armed self-defense to such an extent that even though defensive gun uses (DGUs) are far more common than murders,[6] their reporting favors the latter in an absurd ratio.

Dr. John Lott wrote in 2021: "As of Aug. 10, America's five largest newspapers—the New York Times, Washington Post, Los Angeles Times, USA Today, and the Wall Street Journal—have published a combined total of 10 news stories this year reporting a civilian using a gun to successfully stop a crime, according to a search of the Nexis database of news stories. By contrast, those same newspapers had a total of 1,743 news stories containing the keywords 'murder' or 'murdered' or 'murders' and 'gunfire,' 'shot,' or 'shots.' Including articles with the word 'wounded,' the total rises to 2,764."[7]

They've sold you a lie.

The vulture punditry even attacks prayer now. A horrible thing happens, and people offer their thoughts and prayers. It's just something that decent people do when they can't actively change the situation. But now the vultures won't even allow for that basic human kindness. It's go all in on gun control with them or you are a terrible person.

Hating prayer is particularly ironic, considering all the politicians and reporters *praying* every time there's a shooting that the bad guys turn out to be some right-wing, gun-nut Trump voters. While the vultures actively mock decent people, the anti-gun zealots are the ones exercising faith in the false idols of gun control.

Meanwhile, the gun culture wants all Americans to take advantage of their Second Amendment rights. We think you should go buy guns and get your concealed weapons permits too, that way you can be useful when a psycho decides to shoot up your neighborhood. Oh wait, sorry. Those of you who live in corrupt blue cities don't get to exercise those rights because the politicians you elected want you disarmed so they can feel safe.

They don't care if you get slaughtered as you're helpless and unable to fight back, because then they'll hold a press conference, capitalizing on your death for personal gain before your corpse is even cold.

Wow. Why is it my people are the bad guys again?

■   ■   ■

When former prime minister of Japan, Shinzo Abe, was brutally murdered by an attacker armed with a homemade shotgun constructed out of pipes and a board and held together with electrical tape, President Joe Biden's statement about the killing immediately after the assassination declared that "gun violence always leaves a deep scar on the communities that are affected by it."[8]

In speaking to the press afterwards, he barely expressed perfunctory condolences before rambling off some factually incorrect stats about America's gun crime, and some equally incorrect stats about Japan's lack of murders.[9] As if our two countries aren't an apples-and-oranges comparison. Japan is a super-homogenous society isolated on its own islands, while America is a giant country made up of hundreds of cultures spread across fifty very different states, next door to a narco state with a border our government can't control. I'm pretty sure the Japanese wouldn't have rioted over George Floyd, and if they had, the Japanese police wouldn't have put up with their cities being on fire for months over it. Of course we have different crime rates.

Japan is not us. They've had gun control essentially since the Portuguese introduced firearms there five centuries ago.[10] If Japanese criminals felt like having guns, they'd have them. Their crime is not like our crime. Their organized crime organizations have rules governing civility, and if Japan had a single neighborhood in the entire country half as rowdy as inner-city Baltimore, the Japanese authorities would promptly bulldoze it into the sea. They have a government registry for *swords*. Japan is one of the only countries with a population polite and accommodating enough to accept that level of control.

Despite all that, one scumbag just conclusively demonstrated that even the strictest gun control laws in the world are utterly useless against a determined attacker. And he did it with black powder he probably stole from fireworks, ignited by a battery.

Yet the zealots can't help themselves. They reflexively use the political assassination of a beloved world leader to awkwardly push their current domestic agenda. Because *everything* is about the narrative.

■   ■   ■

As I was editing this manuscript, an event occurred that is a perfect example of the vulture phenomenon. There was an attempted mass shooting at a mall in Greenwood, Indiana. The bad guy was able to kill three before being interrupted by a twenty-two-year-old who was legally carrying a pistol thanks to Indiana's brand-new constitutional carry law. The hero dropped the bad guy before he could hurt anyone else, and the local police labeled him a Good Samaritan. Somehow this story managed to slip past the vulture media and went viral to be seen by the masses.[11]

And the anti-gun zealots lost their minds.

If you care enough to dive into the cesspool of social media, the days following the Good Samaritan's heroic actions provided a profound look at the banality of evil. Don't take my word for it. Go look for yourself. There was an endless parade of butt hurt from the anti-gun camp.

Why were they so outraged that this heroic young man had killed a lunatic before he could murder more innocent people?

It was bad for their narrative.

They were furious that there was a clear example of a "good guy with a gun." That's supposed to be a myth. Sure, we have hundreds of examples where regular armed citizens stopped violent criminals in the act, but the media crushes those in order to keep the public ignorant.

There were pathetic attempts at moral equivalence because the mall had a No Guns Allowed sign. It was supposed to be a gun-free zone, and this armed citizen carried a gun inside anyway! Clearly he's just as big a villain as the mass murderer!

I wish I was exaggerating, but I'm not. One idiot wrote, "This business posted a policy, clearly stating weapons were not allowed on that private property. He violated it just like the shooter did. That is not a 'good Samaritan.'" Another moron (who had PhD after her name) tweeted, "Both the assailant and that 'brave armed citizen' carried weapons into a gun free zone. Hope this young man is charged."[12]

Violating the sanctity of their little No Guns Allowed signs was just as big a sin to them as murder.

A sane and rational person's takeaway from this situation would be that gun-free zones are pointless and everybody else in that mall should be thankful the good guy ignored the signs. Unfortunately for the zealots, Indiana state law says those signs are meaningless suggestions with no force of law behind them anyway. At most, if the person carrying a concealed weapon is seen by management, he can be asked to leave, and failure to do so would constitute trespassing.[13]

So basically you can risk death...or a lifetime ban from Gap. Tough call.

Shannon Watts, spokes-harpy for the astroturf anti-gun organization, Moms Demand Action for Gun Sense in America (which is an incredibly stupid name), was especially upset and wrote, "I don't know who needs to hear this but when a 22-year-old illegally brings a loaded gun into a mall and kills a mass shooter armed with an AR-15 after he already killed three people and wounded others is not a ringing endorsement of our implementation of the Second Amendment."[14]

That sounds like she was upset more people weren't killed. Death is good politics for them. They need higher body counts to cause panic and get votes.

However this vapid creature's tweet helped set the narrative the rest ran with. It was "illegal" for the good guy to be armed. Only it turns out it wasn't, and even if it had been, so what? Aren't innocent lives more important than your stupid, little feel-good sign?

She also seems disturbed the good guy was twenty-two years old, as if that makes any difference.

Her next bit is even more nefarious. She claims that because the bad guy killed several people *before* the good guy could stop him the idea of an armed citizen ending a murderer's spree before the murderer can kill anyone else somehow suspect. The pretzel of spiteful illogic defies untangling. But believe it or not, this take became the narrative of the day.

That's so despicable it makes me want to puke.

We will delve into this in far greater detail later, but it is clear what stops mass killers is a violent response. The faster it is delivered, the better. But even if you are there when it starts, humans still have reaction times. We have to process information in a chaotic situation and then act on it. The aggressor sets the terms, and unless you see them coming, he has the advantage of surprise. Yet it came out that between the moment the bad guy opened fire and the point the Good Samaritan dropped him a mere *fifteen seconds* elapsed.[15]

By any measure this young man did *fantastic*. He outperformed the entire Uvalde PD by himself.

If anybody were crazy enough to follow Shannon Watts's recommendations, the killer wouldn't have had fifteen seconds, he'd have fifteen minutes. Then the vultures could have more blood to dance in.

Remember, armed citizens are like seat belts. They don't prevent crashes. They mitigate damage. Only that's not good enough for Moms Demand Action. It seems like they crave *more death*. That way they can get a bunch of useless laws passed that will disarm the Good

Samaritans and do absolutely nothing to stop the bad guys. They take away the seat belts and say, *That's okay, we'll just declare that cars are no longer allowed to wreck ever again.*

Some of these mopes were even upset that the police called him a Good Samaritan. Because Samaritans are supposed to be meek and nonviolent. I'm sure whoever came up with that narrative is a devout Biblical scholar!

But once it came out that the Good Samaritan (yeah, I'll still call him that—deal with it) hadn't broken any gun-free-zone laws, the narrative quickly shifted to Shannon Watt's dishonest take on how "good guys with guns" are failures because they can't stop the bad guys before they demonstrate they are bad. Well neither can all our laws and the power of the government apparently, so I suppose we should just hang it up then and let them kill as many people as they feel like until the cops arrive.

There was a political cartoon, showing the grim reaper keeping score, with one side filled with hash marks for hundreds of "mass shootings in America" and one single mark under "mass shootings stopped by a good guy with a gun." This was of course immediately shared by lying scumbag reporters spouting nonsense like "348 Mass Shootings in half a year is 348 too many mass shootings. One 'Good Samaritan' doesn't make this ok."[16]

What blatant liars. We've already gone over how they arrive at that ridiculously inflated number, and the "One Good Samaritan" bit is also a preposterous lie. We have hundreds of examples of armed citizens stopping bad guys early in events that *might* have developed into mass shootings, all the way up to events where the aggressor clearly intended to stack as many bodies as possible only to get gunned down before he could reach his goals.

So in the sick, depraved mind of an anti-gun vulture, *everything* counts as a mass shooting, and *nothing* counts as stopping one.

■ ■ ■

Regardless of your politics you really should care about the Second Amendment. In November 2016, a few days after Donald Trump got elected, I wrote an article that went viral titled "A Handy Guide for Liberals Who Are Suddenly Interested in Gun Ownership."[17]

That blog post contained a lot of the same information I've put into this book about how to get armed and trained. My tone was pretty flippant, but in my defense I had gotten rather tired of listening to people who I knew had been vehemently anti-gun their entire lives suddenly shifting gears and histrionically crying about how they were going to arm up in order to battle the second coming of Satan-Hitler before they all got loaded into cattle cars and shipped to the gulag.

Despite my enjoying their wailing and gnashing of teeth, the Second Amendment is for them too, so I did try to provide helpful advice about how to become responsible gun owners. It was rather fun to watch a certain idiotic editor from a big New York City publisher (whom I've known for many years and who has been rabidly anti-gun the entire time) panic and begin sharing gun articles he'd found on the internet with titles like, "What's The Best AR-15 to Buy?" My response was, "None of those, dummy, because every single thing on that list is illegal in New York City and *you* voted to make it that way."

When it comes to the regularly proposed Do-Somethings, whatever your politics, whomever you are voting for this next election, just imagine the hated other side wins. Would you trust their guy with the ability to deprive you of your rights? If you're thinking your sainted choice would never do that, but the crooked, conniving candidate on the other side would totally abuse such a power, then maybe it is a really stupid power to give *anybody*.

In this book we will talk a lot about using firearms for self-defense, but ultimately the Second Amendment is about protecting ourselves from tyranny. This is how I explained it in my handy guide for liberals:

What about Doomsday?

Now the elephant in the room. I've seen a lot of you going on about how terrified you are for all your "marginalized" friends, that the government is going to turn tyrannical and genocidal, and murder them by the million. I don't think that's actually going to happen, but let's say it did. We're talking full on Gestapo-Stasi jack boots and cattle car time. Bear with me through this hypothetical situation, that stuff about ability/opportunity/immediate threat is actually happening, but it is systematically being carried out by agents of the state against its own citizens. I'm talking war in the streets.

I keep seeing you guys saying that you're going to "fight harder." No offense, but bullshit. What are you going to do? Call more innocent bystanders racists? Post more articles from Salon even harder? Have a protest and burn your local CVS? Block more freeways with your bodies? Guess what. If the government has actually gone full tyrannical, they're just going to machine-gun your dumbass in the street. They are going to drive through your roadblock, and your bodies will grease the treads of their tanks.

That's what actual tyrants do. So despite your bitching, virtue signaling, and panic attacks, we're a long way off of that.

There is a saying that has long been common in my half of the country. There are four boxes to be used in defense of liberty: soap, ballot, jury, and ammo. Please use in that order. You can debate, vote, and go to court in order to get things changed. You only go ammo box when those other things no longer work, because once you do, there is no going back.

God willing, America never gets to that point, because if we ever go to war with ourselves again, then it will be a bloodbath the like of which the world has never seen. We have foolishly created a central government so incomprehensibly powerful that to stop it from committing genocide would require millions of capable citizens to rise up and fight.

Congratulations. Now you understand why the Framers put the Second Amendment in there. It is the kill switch on the Republic, and everyone with a clue prays we never have to use it.

Right now you guys are angry and talking a lot of shit. This is all new to you. My side is the one with the guns, training, and the vast majority of the combat vets, and we really don't want our government to get so out of control that this ever happens. Only fools wish for a revolution. But that big red button is still there in case of emergency because if a nation as powerful as America ever turned truly evil then the future is doomed. As Orwell said, "if you want a picture of the future, imagine a boot stamping on a human face—forever."

That's the real meaning of the Second Amendment. So don't screw around with it. If you do, you're no better than the fat wannabes running around the woods in their surplus camo and airsoft plate carriers... You don't get that, but all my gun culture readers know exactly who I'm talking about. They are the morons CNN trots out whenever they need to paint all gun owners as irresponsible, inbred, redneck violent dupes for your benefit.

And spare me the typical talking points about how an AR-15 can't fight tanks and drones...It's way beyond the scope of this article, but you don't have a flipping clue what you're talking about. Every *HuffPo* guest columnist thinks they are von Clausewitz. They aren't.

This Doomsday option is something we never want to use, but which we need to maintain just in case. It is also another reason Hillary lost. One motivator for Americans to vote for Trump was that Hillary hates the Second Amendment. Her husband put the biggest gun ban we've ever had in place, and she has been exceedingly clear that she hates guns and would get rid of all of them if she could.

And doing that would push that big red button.

When the already superpowerful government wants to make you even more powerless, that scares the crap out of regular Americans, but you guys have been all in favor of it. Take those nasty guns! Guns are scary and bad. Don't you stupid rednecks know what's good for you? The people should live at the whim of the state!

But now that the shoe is on the other foot, and somebody you distrust and fear is in charge for a change, the government having all sorts of unchecked power seems like a really bad idea, huh?

Absolute power in the hands of anyone should terrify you. The Second Amendment is there to make sure the foundation of that power always remains in the hands of the people.[18]

■   ■   ■

For a brief and panicked moment, many ardent anti-gunners *almost* got it. They were *so close*. But then within a few weeks they had gone back to barfing up their same tired talking points about how only the police are trained enough to have guns and all of us dumb peasants should be disarmed for our own safety because the state will take care of us...and ironically they wrote all that while they had *#resist* added to their names.

You can't sway the willfully ignorant, but you can defeat them.

Chapter Two

We've all been there.

You're surfing your phone, watching TV, or listening to the radio, and there it is... breaking news. A horrifying crime has happened somewhere. It might be close, but it is probably far. If you're really unlucky, it's someplace you know, filled with people you love. The details are fuzzy. The details are *always* fuzzy at this point. All you know right then is somebody did something terrible and some number of innocent people have been hurt or killed because of it. With growing horror you'll process the details as they come in.

A few things inevitably happen.

Regular people will be shocked and dismayed. Decent folks with good intentions will be disgusted that this horrible crime happened and ask, *How? How could we allow this?* Then they will reflexively demand that somebody *do something*.

The worst among us always see this as an opportunity for political gain. The facts don't matter to them. It is simple stimulus and response. There's a tragedy, so they're going to capitalize on it for their benefit. They'll certainly offer a *something*. Unfortunately the thing they offer usually wouldn't have prevented the crime, it punishes those

21

who had nothing to do with it, and actually makes the problem worse by paving the way for more awful events in the future.

Then there's my people, the so-called *gun culture*. We aren't allowed time to process the event. We don't get the benefit of the proverbial seventy-two-hour rule to wait for all the facts to come in. It doesn't even matter how close the tragedy was to us either. We have to immediately go on defense because we have learned the hard way that if we don't we will have our rights stripped because of someone else's crimes.

The political vultures know they have to push while emotions are high and facts are low. They prey on your desire to feel safe by offering simplistic solutions that put everyone in more danger, while those of us who try to stop them are labeled every horrible thing imaginable. We must want children to die, we're only motivated by the vilest and stupidest impulses, and so on.

Once the facts come in and more is known about the evil doers' tools, tactics, or motivations, if the narrative no longer benefits the control freaks, it quietly vanishes from the news, to never be mentioned again. If it is of use, or can be somehow twisted to be useful, the story will be flogged endlessly until they either get some political mileage out of it or they find some new outrage to fixate on.

Everybody hates each other, while the violent criminals we'd all like to stop keep on doing their thing. It's an ugly cycle, and it never, ever stops.

Americans argue about the Second Amendment and gun control passionately, but many do so ignorantly. The opportunists lie in order to manipulate you. That's not meant as an insult. You don't know what you don't know.

I'd like to fix that.

If you saw something on the news about guns or gun laws, it is probably wrong somehow, misleading at best, or an outright fabrication at worst. It's like listening to a vegan tell you how to properly cook a steak. I'm going to address all of the usual talking points and explain the flaws inherent in each of them.

I strongly believe in our inalienable right to keep and bear arms. My goal is to explain why I came to these conclusions in a manner that is clear, concise, and hopefully of use to you. I won't lie, I'd like this book to give ammo to the people on my side of the debate. To those of you who are on the fence, undecided, I want to help you understand more about how crime and gun control laws actually work. For any readers who are vehemently anti-gun, I hope that you read this with an open mind, because the Second Amendment is truly for everyone. However, when it comes to religious zealots, experience has taught me not to get my hopes up.

This book isn't intended for policy wonks and pundits. I'm not an academic. I'm not a statistician. I'm a writer who knows a lot about guns.

I've been having this exact same argument for my entire adult life. It's not an exaggeration when I say that I know pretty much exactly every single thing an anti-gun activist is going to say before they say it. I've heard it over and over, the same old tired stuff, trotted out every single time there's a tragedy on the news that can be milked. Yet I always get sucked in, spending days arguing with people who either mean well but are uninformed about gun laws and how guns actually work (whom I don't mind at all), or the willfully ignorant (whom I do mind), or the obnoxious types who are completely incapable of any critical thinking deeper than an internet meme (them I can't stand).

A little background for those of you who aren't familiar with my work (and this is going to be extensive so feel free to skip the next few paragraphs), but I need to establish the fact that I know what I am talking about, because I'm sick and tired of my opinion carrying the same weight as the opinions of people who learned everything they know about guns and violence from watching TV.

I am currently a full-time, professional novelist. However, before that I owned a gun store. We were a Title 7 SOT (Special Occupational Taxpayer), which means we worked with legal machine guns, suppressors, and pretty much everything except for explosives. We did law enforcement sales and worked with equipment that's unavailable from most dealers, which meant lots of government inspections and compliance paperwork. I had to be exceedingly familiar with federal gun laws, and there are a multitude of those. I worked with many companies in the gun industry and still have friends and contacts at various manufacturers. When I hear people tell me the gun industry is unregulated, I have to resist the urge to laugh in their faces.

I was also a Utah concealed weapons instructor and one of the busiest in the state. That required me to learn about self-defense laws, and, because I took my job very seriously, I sought out every bit of information I could. My classes were longer than the standard Utah class, and all of that extra time was spent on "use of force," "shoot/ no shoot" scenarios, and role-playing through violent encounters. I have certified thousands of people to carry guns. I've worked as a firearms instructor and have taught students how to shoot defensively with handguns, shotguns, and rifles. I started out as an assistant for some extremely experienced teachers, and over the years I've had the opportunity to take classes from some of the most accomplished experts in the world.

I have been a competition shooter in USPSA (United States Practical Shooting Association), IDPA (International Defensive Pistol Association), and 3-gun matches. During those years it wasn't odd for me to reload and shoot one thousand rounds in any given week. I'm no champion—those people are on an entirely different level—but I've won matches, and I've been able to shoot with some of the top competitive shooters in the country. I'm a fairly capable shooter, but

I only put this part here to convey that I know how shooting works better than the vast majority of the populace.

I've written for national publications on topics relating to gun laws and use of force. I wrote for everything from the United States Concealed Carry Association to *S.W.A.T.* magazine. On a few occasions, I was brought in to testify before the Utah State Legislature on the ramifications of proposed gun laws. I've argued this stuff with lawyers, professors, professional lobbyists, and once made a state rep cry.

Basically, for most of my life, I have been up to my eyeballs in guns, self-defense instruction, and the laws relating to those things. So believe me when I say that I've heard every argument relating to gun control possible. It is pretty rare for me to hear something unique, and none of the arguments are truly new.

Whenever there's a mass killing, politicians will immediately demand that we have a "national conversation on guns." Except these conversations are inevitably a one-sided lecture, where they give us their usual list of demands, while ignoring any solutions we provide that might actually make a difference.

■　　■　　■

Arm Teachers

For example, whenever there is a school shooting and politicians predictably demand we have a "national conversation on guns," no one on their side of this "national conversation" is willing to entertain allowing teachers to carry concealed weapons. This isn't a conversation at all, it's a lecture.

When I suggest letting school employees carry concealed weapons in an article or on social media, I immediately get a bunch of emotional freak-out responses. *You can't mandate teachers be armed! Guns in every classroom! Emotional response! Blood in the streets!*

No. Hear me out. The single best way to stop a mass killer is with an immediate, violent response. Ideally, somebody shoots them dead before they cause too much damage. Often as soon as the killer meets serious resistance, it bursts his fantasy world bubble. Then he retreats, kills himself, or surrenders. This happens over and over again.

Police can be great. I love working with cops. However, any honest cop will tell you that when seconds count, the police are only minutes away. After Columbine the doctrine changed. It used to be that the police took up a perimeter and waited for overwhelming force before going in. Now the standard training across the nation is that if there is an active shooter, you go in. You move toward the sound of gunfire. Every second counts. The longer the shooter has to operate, the more innocents die. You engage rapidly and decisively. If you die, oh well, that's the job you signed up for.

That's the doctrine. That's what cops are supposed to and usually do...But then you've got things like Uvalde. Where they did *everything* wrong. At the time of writing this, the police response is still being investigated, but from what is available to the public right now, their response was pathetic, inept cowardice.

Before Uvalde raised the bar on god-awful police responses, there was the infamous Coward of Broward, where the school resource officer, by all appearances, waited outside where it was safe while the kids he was supposed to be protecting got massacred inside. Seventeen people died while the man who was sworn to protect them did nothing.[1]

Thankfully screwups of that magnitude are rare. I know plenty of cops who have rolled up on situations like this and run toward the sound of gunfire without hesitation because it was the right thing to do. However, even cops like that can't be everywhere. There are at best only a couple hundred thousand on duty at any given time patrolling our entire gigantic country. Excellent response time is in the three-to-five-minute range. We've seen what bad guys can do in three minutes, but sometimes they've got longer. Cops can't teleport. In some cases that means the killer can have ten, fifteen, even twenty minutes to do horrible things with nobody effectively fighting back.

Or an hour-plus if you live somewhere with cancerous institutional rot, where your police force is made up of cowardly trash.

Many schools have a school resource officer. That's a sworn officer, and his sacred duty is protecting the lives of kids no matter what. But talk to any honest cop and he'll give you the long list of problems with that job. Sometimes you get somebody dedicated and sharp, other times that's where departments dump their low performers. That's not even getting into the fact that since school shootings are incredibly rare statistical anomalies, most of that SRO's time is going to be spent distracted by additional duties, like DARE, searching lockers, bugging the juvenile delinquents, and in some cases being a designated babysitter. Even if you do have a quality human being as your SRO, how much ground is he covering? In some cases, how many separate *campuses* is he covering, spread out over how much area?

So if a cop isn't there instantly, what can we do?

According to one calculation, the average number of people shot in an event when the shooter is stopped by responding law enforcement is 14.3. The average number of people shot in an attempted mass killing event when the attacker is stopped by regular people is 2.3.[2]

The reason is simple. The armed citizens are there when it starts.

Teachers are already present. The school staff is already there. Their reaction time is measured in seconds, not minutes. They can serve as your immediate, violent response. Best-case scenario, they engage, shoot, and drop the attacker. A good outcome is this response bursts the attacker's fantasy bubble, and he retreats or commits suicide. Worst-case scenario, the armed staff provides a distraction, and while the bad guy is concentrating on killing them, he's not killing more children.

But teachers aren't as trained as police officers! True, yet totally irrelevant. The teachers don't need to be SWAT cops or Navy SEALs. They need to be speed bumps.

This argument leads to the inevitable shrieking and straw-man arguments about guns in the classroom from the pacifistic-minded who simply can't comprehend themselves being mandated to carry a gun, or those who believe teachers are all too incompetent and can't be trusted. Let me address both at one time.

Don't make it mandatory. Make it entirely voluntary.

That's it. The only people who are worth a damn with a gun are the ones who wish to take responsibility and carry a gun.

Carrying a lethal weapon is not for everyone. There's no shame in taking a realistic look at your mindset and capabilities and saying, *Nope, that's not the best choice for me.* Maybe weapons stress you out. Or you know you're a klutz. That's fine. You're being honest and responsible. If you are a teacher, but the idea of shooting someone is inconceivable to you, or you hate guns and have zero desire to learn to use one well, then this is *definitely* not for you.

However, there are some other employees at your school who would do fine, so get out of their way.

A school employee with a concealed handgun who is a few yards down the hall is a lot more useful in this kind of emergency than a cop who is a mile away. Supporting a policy of allowing your coworkers to be armed might someday save your life. And far more importantly, it might save the lives of the kids in your care.

This is rather simple to implement. Parents and teachers just need to convince their state legislature to make it so that their state's concealed weapons laws trump the federal Gun-Free School Zones Act (which was part of the Joe Biden–sponsored Crime Control Act of 1990[3]). All that means is that teachers who voluntarily decide to get a concealed weapons permit are capable of carrying their guns at work. Easy. Simple. Cheap. Available now.

Some will always say that this is impossible and then present all sorts of terrible worst-case scenarios about the horrors that will happen with a gun in the classroom. But guess what? Some states already do this and have for a long time. My state, Utah, allows for somebody with a concealed weapons permit to carry a gun in a school right now, and has done so for well over a decade.

When I was a CCW instructor, I decided that I wanted more teachers with skin in the game, so I started a program where I would teach anybody who worked at a school for free. No charge. They still had to pay the state for their background check and fingerprints, but all the instruction was free. I wanted more armed teachers in my state.

I personally taught several hundred teachers and quickly discovered that pretty much every single school had at least one competent, capable, smart, willing individual. Some schools had more. I had one high school where the principal, three teachers, and a janitor showed up for class. They had just had an event where there had been a threat against the school and their resource officer had turned up AWOL. This had been a wake-up call for this principal that they were on their own, and he had taken it upon himself to talk to his teachers to find the willing and capable. Good for them.

After the shooting at Virginia Tech, I started teaching college students for free as well. These were adults who could pass a background check. Why should they have to be defenseless? None of my students ever needed to stop a mass killer, but they did shoot a few rapists and robbers, so I consider my time well spent.

Over the course of a couple years, I taught over $20,000 worth of free CCW classes. It was the least I could do. I got to meet hundreds of teachers, students, and staff. All of them were responsible adults who understood that they were stuck in target-rich environments filled with defenseless innocents. Whether they liked it or not, they were the first line of defense.

Other Utah instructors did this as well, with the biggest CCW classes ever taught in our state being made up entirely of teachers.

Back when I was teaching, Utah was an anomaly. Since then many other states have changed their laws to allow for legal CCW in schools, and I believe we are now up to nine that specifically allow for armed school staff in some capacity.[4] If your state is not one of those, and you are sincere in your wish to protect our children, I would suggest you call your state rep today and demand that the state allow concealed carry in schools.

These policies are not implemented equally in every state. There are many anti-gun zealots working in education who like to throw up roadblocks. In my own state, we had years of court and legislative battles over this, with various school districts and public universities flaunting the law until they were soundly defeated. Texas forbids CCW in schools, but it does have a specific program where a teacher can be armed, though this requires permission of the school board. As you can imagine, not all school boards are created equal.

That kind of regulation is foolish. The only rules schools—or any employer really—need to add to their employee handbook about CCW are these: If you are going to legally carry a gun at work, keep it concealed at all times, keep it securely on your person at all times, and only pull it out for matters of life or death, or we fire your ass. Simple. You don't need to overcomplicate this with extra paperwork, bureaucratic oversight, or mandatory training.

Armed teachers aren't the surefire cure for school shootings, but they can help. No one single thing is going to make a place totally secure. It is about "defense in depth." Multiple layers of security, working together. If one fails, hopefully the next stops the threat. Your car has brakes, lights, and mirrors to avoid collisions, but you also wear a seat belt for when you can't. It is even better if your car has the additional level of airbags. And so on.

This is the same thing. Armed staff members are a layer. SROs and responding cops are a layer. Things like heavy-duty doors and controlled entrances can be a layer. Training in situational awareness so the staff knows what to look for could be a layer. Wishful thinking and laws that don't actually accomplish anything are *not* a layer. Law enforcement members actually investigating dozens of tips about somebody planning an attack would be a great layer, if they actually got around to it. Systems fail, which is why we build in redundancies.

Anything that delays, distracts, or interrupts a mass murderer is worth its weight in gold.

This isn't just about those apocalyptic scenarios either. In 2021 there was an attempted kidnapping in Ogden, Utah, where a man tried to snatch an eleven-year-old girl from an elementary school playground. There was no apparent link between the kidnapper and the child either, he just decided to take her. Thankfully a heroic teacher—who was legally carrying a concealed weapon—stopped the kidnapper and held him at gunpoint until the police arrived.[5]

I've had people tell me that they don't like the idea of teachers carrying concealed because they know some teachers who are flakes, and we've got plenty of TikTok videos of weirdos to prove this point. However, teachers are individuals just like in any other career field. There's good and bad, smart and dumb, worth a damn or useless. I have a friend who is a substitute teacher who also happens to be a retired Green Beret. He's calm, professional, experienced, and better in a gunfight than 99.9 percent of the cops who might respond to that 911 call. Why wouldn't you want someone like him armed in your kid's school?

Last and most important: If you are one of these school employees who carries at work, you have a responsibility to be as trained and capable as your circumstances allow. Everybody who carries a gun does, but you're entrusted with other people's children. You can't phone this in. Get trained. Practice. Don't get stagnate. Keep learning and improving.

Be the best speed bump you can be.

Chapter Three

Create Defense in Depth

Self-defense is a human right. Every individual being able to protect himself from harm is a fundamental principle of our society. Everyone should be entitled to this right without discrimination. The state doesn't have a monopoly on force. We delegate that responsibility to them with the understanding that they'll administer the laws equitably. Those laws should *never* require us to be defenseless. Enforced helplessness is tyranny.

When evil attacks, you can either be in a position to do something about it, or you can wait and hope for help. Sometimes you are on your own. Nobody is coming to save you. Would you rather have a chance and fight back or hide under your desk and pray to God that you're not the next one to die?

If your answer is hide and pray, that's fine—for you. That's your choice. But *we* are not *you*. Every one of us has a different level of skill, knowledge, ability, courage, and commitment. What's the right choice for you is not necessarily the right decision for anyone else. You don't get to make that decision for others. If you aren't willing to fight, that's okay, but you don't speak for the rest of us, so please get out of our way.

Being armed and trained doesn't guarantee your safety any more than wearing a seat belt ensures you'll live through a crash or owning a fire extinguisher means your house won't burn down, yet those tools often help prevent tragedies, or at least keep a bad problem from becoming worse.

This debate tends to focus on two different types of crime, the far more common regular criminal who sometimes uses violence or the threat of violence to reach his goals, and the more terrible, yet much rarer, mass killers, who get disproportionate media attention.

As we've seen constantly demonstrated, the best way to end a mass killer event is with an immediate, violent response. If that response comes from somebody already present, the body count will be lower. If the response comes from the authorities, then there are usually more casualties simply due to the response time.

No one is naïve enough to think that merely having a regular person with a gun nearby is a perfect solution. Permit holders have been murdered in these events too. There have been mass killings where there were armed guards present, but the attacker still got through. Guards have a purpose. They keep the riffraff out, but when you are dealing with a motivated killer, a lone posted guard is also an obvious first target.

This is where the concept of "defense in depth" comes into play. Security is made up of multiple layers. If one layer fails, hopefully the next one intercepts the threat. Each layer the attacker has to go through buys time and complicates his mission. IT departments don't just rely on a firewall. They've got layers of security: passwords, software patches, policies, and a physical lock on the server room door. In a warzone, the military doesn't just arm the troops on the front line, because the enemy will try to go around where you are strongest, to hit the vulnerable areas behind them. Which is why rear echelon support troops are also armed, so the attackers will always meet resistance.

Too many of the Do-Somethings assume that if we ban a particular thing, the bad guy will be thwarted and stop. Real life shows us that threats always find a way around. If you've got an armed guard on some facility, that's just one level of defense. They go around. You ban some gun, they get it anyway. You got a secure door, and they drive their car into your lobby. You violate the civil rights of millions to red-flag one actual bad guy? He reassesses and makes a new plot. Like water flowing downhill, evil gets around.

Whether you want to be or not, *you* are a layer of defense. And unfortunately, you might be the *first* layer, and you might be the *only* layer available.

You can either accept this reality and prepare, or you can hope misfortune passes you by.

When Regular People Fight Back

We've all seen that guy who says, "I've never needed a gun. Nothing bad has ever happened to me. I just don't go to bad places. You're paranoid."

Fool.

He has never needed a gun...yet. Nothing bad has ever happened to him, but he's not you. He doesn't go to "bad places," but some of you live there, and even if you don't, sometimes the bad place comes to you. Evil delivers.

Naïve wishful thinkers go through life oblivious and insist that you do too. If you understand the horrors that man has routinely inflicted on man, and recognize that history repeats itself, they'll call you paranoid. They realize there are bad people in the world, but they've abdicated their responsibilities to the state, hoping the state will protect them and assuming men with badges are the only level of defense needed to keep them safe from harm.

They think their good intentions will get them safely through life. Sadly the bad guys have a vote in the matter too. And when you talk to these oblivious types after they get victimized—assuming they survived—they'll say something like, "I couldn't believe it was happening to me!"

A lot of bad actors are stopped by the state. The feds bust a terrorist cell. The cops roll up a psycho plotting mayhem. Except somebody will always inevitably get through those official state layers. Not to mention the many times we have heard the frustrating words "the attacker was known to law enforcement" and he went on to kill anyway.

The next line of defense is whichever unlucky bastards happen to be in the way.

Even then, nuts-and-bolts reality, once the attack is happening, our "good guy with a gun" may or may not be in a position to help. Gun fights are chaotic. Each one unfolds differently. You can do everything right and still die. You can screw up, get lucky, and live. But ultimately guns are the only tools that provide options you would not otherwise have.

When regular people do fight back, they become an obstacle and a complication. At minimum killers are slowed down. At best, the threat is neutralized. Rational people consider this a victory.

Anti-gun activists will often declare that our proverbial "good guy with a gun" is a myth. PBS calls it "a deadly American fantasy."[1] In fact, if you do a search for "good guy with a gun," you will get page after page of results from newspapers and magazines that all share a hard-left slant, declaring that there's no such thing.[2]

Claiming the "good guy with a gun" to be a myth is a perfect example of sleazy, manipulative journalism, because if the attacker is stopped early, then technically he never achieved the body count necessary for it to be counted as a mass shooting. If the bad guy had already managed to shoot enough people before some regular person was able to blast him, then technically that mass shooting already happened. So even though an untold number of lives were spared by the good guy stopping it sooner, it doesn't count. It's a catch-22.

The media actually doesn't care if you live or die. Only their narrative matters.

Yet there are so many examples of regular armed people who happened to be nearby stopping a killer in the act that these reporters are either blatantly lying on purpose or they are profoundly, willfully ignorant. I know how I'd bet.

In Texas in 2019, a shotgun-wielding madman opened fire on a church congregation. He was able to kill two before a permit holder drew his concealed handgun and ended the bad guy's life.[3]

How much worse could it have been if that regular citizen with a gun hadn't been in that church? *Much worse.* As demonstrated two years earlier, when a gunman was able to kill twenty-six inside another Texas church. What stopped that one? Another armed citizen who lived nearby heard the gunfire, grabbed his rifle, and bolted out of his home *barefoot* to challenge the attacker. After the attacker was hit in the torso and leg, he fled in his vehicle. The barefoot hero then flagged down a motorist, and they pursued the attacker while giving directions to 911. When the bad guy wrecked, the two good guys took up a defensive position until the cops arrived five minutes later to find the bad guy dead of a self-inflicted gunshot wound.[4]

What stops killers? A violent response. The only real question is how long it takes to arrive.

The identity of the responder doesn't matter. It could be a regular Joe, an off-duty cop, or the British SAS. What matters is that there is a response as soon as possible. Best-case scenario the good guy puts the killer down fast, but even if that doesn't happen, once the killer has to fight, he is at minimum distracted from murdering the helpless.

Encountering resistance might even make him decide this isn't what he'd hoped for and give up, or do us all a favor and blow his own brains out.

The important thing is how much time elapses between the beginning of the event and the violent response. That's the time the killer is allowed to work unimpeded.

Despite the media claiming good guys with a gun are a myth, we have a multitude of examples of regular citizens using guns to defend themselves, and specifically we have examples of them stopping mass killings that were already in progress. As for how many events were stopped before they reached the level of being considered a mass shooting, that's really difficult to estimate, because it's hard to tell how many more people a killer might have killed if he hadn't gotten plugged first.

The Crime Prevention Research Center has done a great job compiling news stories from around the country where regular citizens used their guns to stop mass killers or events that likely would have turned into mass killings. They have compiled over *eighty* incidents, and their list can't be considered comprehensive either because of how little coverage the media gives to this topic.[5]

In Charleston, West Virginia, a man with a rifle began firing into a graduation party. A woman who was legally carrying a pistol immediately shot and killed him. This happed the day after Uvalde. This woman was saving lives while the media was crowing about how people like her are a myth.[6]

Note, that compilation I mention is only for events that were or likely would have been mass killings. The Crime Prevention Research Center compiles regular defensive gun uses separately, recording dozens of local news reports for separate incidents *per month*.[7]

Peace through Preparedness

I've had buffoons sanctimoniously lecture me that by talking about this I must want people to live in fear. Quite the contrary, I want people to go about living their lives in peace, equipped with the tools to survive in the off chance something terrible happens. I buy health insurance and smoke alarms, but I don't live my life in constant fear of disease or fire. With proper training and practice, you can conceal a handgun as easily as you carry your car keys or cell phone. Wearing it just becomes part of your routine.

Don't let someone shame you for understandable worries. Fear is normal and we have it for a reason. The problem is irrational fear that causes you to make bad decisions. You are right to fear violent crime because it clearly exists. That's perfectly rational. Disarming all the potential victims because you are afraid one of them might potentially do something harmful is irrational.

Mass killings are a statistical anomaly. The odds of your being involved in one are minuscule. You are far more likely to be a victim of regular, good old-fashioned, non-newsworthy violent crime, and in those cases a gun is a very useful tool to have. Despite breathless media coverage to the contrary, our murders had been trending downward for decades until the great national temper tantrum of 2020.[8]

Now some of you might be thinking this is spin. Surely these events must be more common. They are on the news constantly.

Originally, "mass shooting" was a specific law enforcement term reserved for killers operating with the specific goal of taking many lives. The school shooters, the disgruntled office killers, the maniacs who shoot up the mall, the psychos who want to destroy your world—that's how most people rightfully think of the term. The number of those so far this year is more like seven or eight, not three or four hundred. Even one is awful, but the vultures can only arrive at that massively inflated number by torturing the definition to include any event where multiple people get hit by bullets. Some drug dealers start blasting each other over who gets to sell drugs on a specific corner—mass shooting. If somebody accidentally pulls the trigger on a hunting rifle and the bullet hits the floor so that fragments scratch three people—mass shooting.

Statistical rarity aside, bad things will continue to happen. No amount of symbolic—ultimately useless—laws will change that. When these bad things happen, you can either be in a position to deal with them effectively, or not.

In an attempt to minimize the usefulness of firearms, there have been some outlandish ideas bandied about for alternatives. I once had another novelist tell me that his favorite tool for self-defense was his cell phone. This was a particularly ironic statement since he declared it during the aftermath of the Pulse nightclub shooting where *the killer* called 911 beforehand.[9] But my friend figured that to prevent a violent crime all you had to do was take the bad guy's picture and store it, and then he wouldn't dare do anything bad to you because he'd get caught—that was such a goofy idea that it took me a moment to process the magnitude of the naïveté. Banks have cameras, yet they still get robbed. There are plenty of regular violent criminals who film themselves assaulting people for fun. In the case of most mass killers, they want infamy and are trying to send some kind of message, so they'll probably smile for the camera, then wait for you to upload it to Instagram before shooting you in the face.

They are not like you.

Gun Control Is a Bait-and-Switch Tactic

Gun control isn't about guns, it's about control. Power-hungry charlatans make it about the tools they want to regulate, yet evil men have killed with fire, fertilizer, cars, and even airliners. They've used guns to kill with impunity in countries where only the government was supposed to have guns, and the only difference between those places and here was the time that elapsed before the violent response.

Evil men will continue to kill because that's what they do.

Global geopolitics are out of your hands. Curing the societal problems that create monsters are beyond your control. Most of us can't do crap about the sad state of the entire world. What we *can* do right now is see to ourselves, our loved ones, and our immediate surroundings.

If you decide to carry a gun, remember you're not a cop, you're not some junior danger-ranger or self-appointed sheep dog. You have no obligation to get involved in someone else's business, and in fact doing so can get you killed or in legal trouble. This stuff is not the time for bravado. You need to do a cold, hard, realistic assessment of your capabilities. If you don't have the right mindset, or you don't think you could shoot somebody, don't. This isn't for everybody. However, there are millions of regular men and women who can, and history has demonstrated that they will protect themselves and others if they're allowed to.

In the aftermath of any event that brings the gun rights debate back up, there's always someone claiming that armed citizens "would have just made it worse." It doesn't even matter what the event was, they'll even declare that about situations that were stopped by a regular person who clearly *didn't* make it worse.

There's always cowardly projection after a shooting makes the news. "You'd freak out and shoot the wrong person!" Except that rarely happens. In fact, mistaken identity shootings happen with police officers far more often than they do with armed citizens, just because the cops have to respond and figure out who is who, while the armed citizen was usually there when it started so there's no question who was in need of shooting.

In Arvada, Colorado, in 2021, a good guy with a gun stopped a cop-killer on a rampage. After the bad guy was shot, the hero was then tragically gunned down by another responding police officer by mistake.[10] The only thing that's consistent about gunfights is that they're going to suck for somebody, but this is the only case that I'm aware of where a good guy with a gun saved the day and then got mistakenly shot by the police.

The tired "you'd just make things worse" is even more obnoxious when it is invoked for situations that are so horrific that all you can ask is *how*. It's already a blood-soaked massacre. Heaven forbid somebody shoot back!

The thing that makes these events worse is the *lack of response*. Uvalde PD owns arguably the greatest failure in the history of American law enforcement because they didn't act. I've actually seen people saying Uvalde's inept cowardice proves that there is no such thing as a good guy with a gun. No, you dolts, there were good guys with guns there, and the police *stopped them*.[11]

I do find one thing tragically amusing about the debate over CCW. In my personal experience, some of the most vehemently anti-gun people I've ever associated with will, after getting to know me, eventually admit that if something bad happened to them, then they "really hope I'm around because I'm *one of the good ones*." They never realize how hypocritical this sounds. They want to assume the worst about everybody else while remaining convinced their own character is pure as the driven snow. But what they really are after is to keep everyone disarmed and helpless.

Chapter Four

The Usual Somethings

As soon as there is a tragedy, there come the calls of "We have to do something!" Sure, the something may not actually accomplish anything as far as solving whatever the tragedy was or preventing the next one, but that's the narrative. Something evil happened, so we have to do *something*, and preferably we have to do it right now before we think about it too hard.

In an ideal world, gun rights would be a bipartisan issue, as everybody has the right to keep and bear arms to defend themselves, regardless of wealth, race, sex, religion, or social standing. However, that's not how things are currently in our system, with one of our major parties being absolutely in love with gun control, while the other ranges from decent to awful in its defense of the Second Amendment depending on what day of the week it is.

Gun control is extremely unpopular in red-state America, and so it is hard to pass any new state laws there, but there is still a century's accumulation of onerous smaller laws. There have been a handful of major federal laws passed in the United States relating to guns, all of them terrible, yet the majority of really strict gun control has been enacted primarily in blue states and liberal-dominated urban areas. Many of those are an endangered species due to the recent Supreme Court decision *New York State Rifle & Pistol Association, Inc. v. Bruen*, but at the time of writing this, those laws are still in effect. There are a multitude of state and federal gun laws already on the books—and many more regulations from federal agencies concerning the manufacturing and sale of firearms.

A fundamental consistency to all historic gun control is that those laws were designed to keep weapons out of the hands of "undesirables." In the old days, they could be more blatant about who they wanted disarmed, whether it was freed slaves, American Indians, whatever the hated group of immigrants was at the time, or just poor people in general. Gun laws were always about controlling whatever group the elite, respectable levels of society found distasteful. Meanwhile, those rich and politically connected enough were always left with a workaround, or the laws simply weren't enforced against them at all.

As we will see going through the modern laws, not much has changed in that respect.

The average American is uneducated about what gun laws already exist, what those actually do, and even the fundamental terminology of the laws. So I'm going to go through the Do-Somethings that are usually suggested and try to break everything down. I'll leave out the particularly crazy ones I've been confronted with, like the guy who was in favor of putting "automatic robot gun turrets" in schools— because of course somebody who is appalled at the idea of teachers being able to voluntarily carry a concealed weapon at work is in favor of mandating killer robots.

"We Need to Ban Automatic Weapons!"

Okay. Done. America pretty much did that back in 1934. The National Firearms Act of 1934 made it so that you had to pay a $200 tax on a machine gun and register it with the government. Adjusting for inflation, that would be about $4,000 now. Like most gun laws, the NFA was racist and classist in nature, as the wealthy could still afford to buy machine guns, but regular people could not. In 1986 that NFA registry was closed, and there have been no new legal machine guns manufactured for civilians to own since then.

"Automatic," "full-auto," or "machine gun" means that when you hold down the trigger, the gun keeps on shooting until you let go or run out of ammo. Because of the artificially limited supply, actual legal machine guns cost a lot of money. The cheapest one you can get right now starts around $5,000, and they go up astronomically from there because they are all basically collector's items. Plus you need to jump through extra hoops to purchase one, including waiting for approval from the BATFE (Bureau of Alcohol, Tobacco, Firearms, and Explosives—but I'm just going to call them the ATF for the rest of the book because the full acronym is ridiculous), and you are only able to transfer them through a special type of dealer. To the best of my knowledge, there has only ever been one crime committed with an NFA-registered machine gun in my lifetime, and in that case the perp was a cop.[1]

Now are machine guns still used in crimes? Why, yes, they are. The actual number of *illegal* machine guns in the United States is impossible to estimate. To hammer home the point: Illegal means it is against the law to possess one of these. Criminals either make or convert their own (which is not hard to do at all), or the machine guns are smuggled into the country—usually by the same people who are able to smuggle in hundreds of tons of drugs—and criminals use them simply because criminals, by definition, don't obey the law.

In 2019 "ATF and customs officials identified more than 2,900 packages" that had been shipped in from China with the parts necessary to build illegal machine guns,[2] and if you think this one operation that got caught is the only one that's ever done this, I've got some really bad news for you.

So even an item that has been banned for the most part since my grandparents were kids—and hasn't been manufactured since I was in elementary school—still ends up in the hands of any criminal who really wants one. Another fantastic example of how well government bans work.

When the news says, "automatic," most people think machine guns, but what they most probably mean by that is semi-automatic.

"Okay. We Need to Ban Semi-Automatic Weapons!"

Semi-automatic means that each time you pull the trigger the action cycles and loads another round. This is the single most common type of gun, not just in America, but in the whole world. Almost all handguns are semi-automatic. The vast majority of weapons used for self-defense are semi-automatic, as are almost all the weapons used by police officers. It is the most common because it is normally the most effective.

Semi-automatic is usually the best choice for defensive purposes. It is easier to use because you can do so one-handed if necessary and you are forced to manipulate your weapon less. If you believe that using a gun for self-defense is necessary, then you pretty much have to say that semi-auto is okay.

Banning semi-automatics basically means banning all guns. I'll get to the issues around that big ask later.

"We Should Ban Handguns!"

Handguns are useful tools for self-defense, and the only reason we use them over the more capable and easier-to-hit-with rifles or shotguns is that handguns are portable. Rifles are just plain better, but I don't carry an AR-15 around because it would be hard to hide under my shirt.

A concealed carry firearm is a wonderful self-defense tool. As much as it offends some people and we keep hearing horror stories about hypothetical shoot-outs between road-raging permit holders, the fact is that over my lifetime most of the United States enacted some form of concealed carry law, and the blood-in-the-streets Wild West shootouts over parking spaces that were predicted simply haven't happened. There have only been a few holdouts, all of them blue states with large cities that suffer from terrible crime, where only the rich and politically connected are allowed to carry guns and the criminals simply don't care and use them anyway.

In fact, this experiment has gone so well over the last couple of decades that fully half of the states have now enacted what is called "constitutional carry," where regular law-abiding citizens can carry a gun in public without even needing a permit. And those handful of holdout states were recently smacked down when the Supreme Court ruled their bigoted concealed carry laws to be unconstitutional.[3]

CCW works. Just like banning semi-automatics basically means banning all guns, banning handguns is actually a declaration that people have no right to defend themselves outside of their homes. You can see why that is a hard sell.

"We Should Ban Assault Rifles!"

Define "assault rifle."

Uh…

Yeah. That's the problem. The term "assault rifle" gets bandied around a lot. Politically, the term is a loaded-nonsense one that picked up steam back during the Clinton years. It was one of those tricks where you name legislation something catchy, like PATRIOT Act, which was another law rammed through while emotions were high and nobody was thinking, go figure.

To gun experts an assault rifle is a very specific type of weapon that originated for the most part in the 1940s. It is a magazine-fed, select-fire (meaning capable of full-auto), intermediate-cartridge (as in, relatively not that powerful) infantry weapon. Real assault rifles in the United States have been heavily regulated since before they were invented because of the NFA of 1934.

For the media and politicians, "assault rifle" is basically a catchall term for any gun that looks scary. I've had people get mad at me because they said that the term had entered common usage, so we should all know what they mean. Sure, but if you intend to legislate it, you have to define it.

Which brings us back to the fact that it's a nonsense term. The U.S. had an assault weapons ban once before. It was signed into law in 1994, lasted for a decade, and was utterly useless. I mean, it was totally, literally pointless. The DOJ commission to study it admitted that it accomplished absolutely nothing.[4]

Really all the AWB did was tick a bunch of normal Americans off, and as a result we bought *a lot* more guns.

To enact the Assault Weapons Ban, politicians had to define the term; and since the real version of an assault weapon didn't actually exist here in any meaningful quantities, they decided to make a list of features, and if your gun possessed a couple of these, then it became an evil assault weapon and was thus banned. The problem was none of these features actually made the gun functionally any different or somehow more lethal or better than any other run-of-the-mill firearm. Most of the criteria were so silly that they became a huge joke to gun owners, except of course, for that portion of gun owners who were otherwise law-abiding citizens but accidentally became instant felons because one of their guns had some cosmetic feature that was now illegal.

One of the criteria was that it was semi-automatic. See above. It is hard to ban the single most common and readily available type of gun in the world, unless you believe in confiscation, but we'll get to that. So they added detachable magazines. That's got to be an Evil Feature, right? And yes, we really did call these Evil Features. I'll talk about magazines below, but once again, it is pretty hard to ban something so incredibly common unless you want to go on a confiscatory national suicide mission.

For example, flash hiders sound dangerous. Let's say having a flash hider makes a gun an assault weapon. So flash hiders became an Evil Feature. Only in reality flash hiders don't do much. They screw onto the end of your muzzle and divert the flash off to the side instead of straight up, so it isn't as annoying when you shoot. It doesn't actually hide the flash from anybody else. EVIL.

Barrel shrouds were listed. Barrel shrouds are just pieces of metal that go over the barrel so you don't accidentally touch the hot part. They became an instantaneous felony too. Collapsible stocks make it so you can adjust your rifle to different-size shooters, that way a tall guy and his short wife can shoot the same gun. Nope. EVIL FEATURE! Pistol grip sounds scary, but it's just a handle. It's simply how you hold it. Having your wrist straight or at an angle doesn't make the weapon any more dangerous.

This nonsense has been a running joke in the gun community ever since the ban passed. When U.S. Representative Carolyn McCarthy was asked by a reporter what a barrel shroud was, she replied, "I think, I believe it's a shoulder thing that goes up."[5] Oh good. I'm glad that thousands of law-abiding Americans unwittingly committed felonies because they had a cosmetic piece of sheet metal on their barrel, which has no bearing whatsoever on crime, but could possibly be a shoulder thing that goes up.

Now are you starting to see why "assault weapons" is a pointless term? They aren't functionally any more powerful or deadly than any normal gun. In fact the cartridges they are normally chambered in are far less powerful than your average deer rifle. Don't worry though, because the same people who fling around the term assault weapons also refer to scoped deer rifles as "high-powered sniper guns," and they'll come for those next.

Basically, what most people are thinking of as assault weapons aren't special.

Despite the panic and hype, rifles are rarely used as murder weapons. In America they have fewer confirmed kills than knives, clubs, or fists. We are talking two or three hundred murders out of our well over ten thousand murders we have every year, in a country with a population of a third of a billion, and more guns in circulation than people.[6] So only two or three hundred murders per year are specifically confirmed as being committed with a rifle according to FBI numbers, and that number is for *all* rifles, with the subset that could be considered assault rifles being even smaller.

Despite that incredibly tiny number, our Congress—which has an approval rating somewhere south of prostate cancer—is once again pushing this same tired crap, and they are just as ignorant as usual about what they are trying to legislate.

The reason that semi-automatic, magazine-fed, intermediate-caliber rifles have become the single most popular type of rifle in America is that they are excellent for many uses, but I'm not talking about fun. I'm talking business. In this case they are excellent for shooting bad people who are trying to hurt you in order to make them stop trying to hurt you. These types of guns are superb defensive weapons, especially in a true Second Amendment sense.

"You Don't Need an Assault Rifle for Hunting!"

Who said anything about hunting? That whole thing about the Second Amendment being for sportsmen is hogwash. As soon as the founding fathers got done fighting a rebellion against the most powerful army in the world, they promptly sat down and codified our all-important right...to hunt deer? Yeah, right. That sounds plausible.

Recreational firearms use is a happy bonus. The Second Amendment is about bearing arms to protect ourselves from threats, up to and including a tyrannical government.

"We Should Ban the AR-15 (or Insert Scary Gun of the Week Here)!"

They say that because the AR-15 is the only rifle they can name. When I was younger, they would have said AK-47 or Uzi instead, because those got mentioned on the news more. If they were arguing to ban handguns, they would say Glock, because it's the most common brand and they've heard its name on TV a lot. Same principle.

An AR-15 is just one type of semi-automatic, magazine-fed rifle like I talked about previously. There is nothing that unique or dangerous about them when compared to any other semi-automatic, magazine-fed rifle. They get used in crimes because they're the most common rifle in America. Reacting in horror to it would be like acting shocked that a criminal drove a Toyota. Only this reaction is even sillier because there are dozens of companies that manufacture AR-15 variants.

"AR" doesn't stand for "Assault Rifle." I don't know how many times I've seen that. It stands for ArmaLite, the company that the designer, Eugene Stoner, worked for when he made the prototype way back in 1956. Yes. The AR is practically a senior citizen. Did you think that this was some sort of bleeding-edge tech? Nope. It's old enough to collect social security.

AR-15s are popular because they're easy to use, modular enough to be configured for many different roles, and yes, fun to shoot. That might offend you, but oh well. Half the country enjoys shooting recreationally.

On that note, the Supreme Court said that the government can't ban arms that are in common use.[7] Despite that, imbecilic elected officials like Jerry Nadler have been dumb enough to argue that they want to ban AR-15s because they *are* so common, in the hopes that once they're banned they won't be common anymore.[8]

"It's a Weapon of War! There's No Reason for Civilians to Ever Have a Weapon of War!"

To really put the icing on the cake, that one needs to come from someone who has Ukrainian flags in their Twitter handle. The same people who cheered while actual assault rifles were being handed out like candy to regular Ukrainian citizens so they could fight back against murderous tyrants now act baffled as to why regular citizens here in the United States want guns.

Technically speaking, no military issues AR-15s. They issue its full-auto-capable military cousin the M-16 or M-4 carbine. But that's just semantic quibbling. We know what you mean. The AR-15 shares a design heritage with a commonly issued military weapon.

Except so do most of the other firearms used in America too, including the most innocuous of sporting guns. The most common bolt-action deer or elk rifles, like the Remington 700 or Winchester Model 70, have military versions used as sniper rifles. The same is the case for most of our popular handguns: A similar version has been issued to some military somewhere. Revolvers have been military issue as recently as Desert Storm. Even the ubiquitous pump-action shotgun, as recommend for home defense by Joe Biden himself,[9] has been a "weapon of war." At one point the Germans even claimed using one of those was a war crime.[10] Americans hunt ducks with them.

The military wants firearms that are reliable, simple, accurate, and affordable—which are the same criteria civilian consumers are looking for. If you are going to get a weapon to defend yourself, why wouldn't you want something similar to the weapons that have already been tested and are known to work in harsh environments? That's a no-brainer.

I've had people tell me that the only purpose for AR-15s is to slaughter the maximum number of people possible as quickly as possible. Uh huh... Which is why every single police department and federal agency in America uses them, because of all that slaughtering cops do daily. Cops use AR-15s for the same reasons we do: they are handy, versatile, and can stop an attacker quickly in a variety of circumstances if necessary.

When I say, "stop an attacker quickly," I've had people on the internet get angry and say, "'Stop.' That's just a euphemism for kill!" Nope. I am perfectly happy if the attacker surrenders or passes out from blood loss too. Tactically and legally, all I care about is making the attacker stop whatever it is that he is doing that caused me to shoot him to begin with.

Ironically, some of our elected officials are so dumb or dishonest—or some combo thereof—that their latest proposed ban on "weapons of war" ignores a bunch of actual, literal weapons of war, including some of the most famous in history, just because they don't look as frightening. There's not a whole lot of logic to this one.

So most of America's firearms are weapons of war? Yes. They can be if necessary. And that's exactly the point. The guns that scare wannabe tyrants the most are common and popular exactly because they are excellent for fighting.

"We Should Ban Hollow Points/Black Talons/'Cop Killer' Ammunition/Armor Piercing/(Insert Scary-Sounding Bullet Here), Because Their Only Purpose Is to Kill!"

I'm dating myself with the Black Talon reference, but it was amusing watching news anchors embarrass themselves by temporarily fixating on one name-brand bullet (which wasn't appreciably different than any other bullet) and then assigning it insane, physics-defying attributes that would be too far-fetched for me to put in a sci-fi novel. No, they aren't miniature whirling saw blades of death, they're just bullets.

Hollow point ammunition is what is commonly used for self-defense, especially in pistol-caliber weapons. Hollow point bullets are designed to expand on impact. Why? Because that slightly larger diameter is more likely to hit something that will cause a faster drop in blood pressure, leading to quicker incapacitation. If you have to shoot somebody who is trying to kill you, the faster he stops trying to kill you the better.

An added benefit to hollow point ammunition is that the mushrooming effect makes the bullet more likely to stop in your target, rather than passing through and retaining enough energy to injure someone on the other side. This is such a no-brainer that I believe every single police department in the country uses some kind of expanding or fragmenting ammunition in their handguns. I'd be shocked if any did otherwise.

Of course, that's what citizens are going to use for regular self-defense too, and we have done so everywhere that hollow points haven't been banned by local laws.

So-called "cop killer" ammunition was just bullets that would go through a bulletproof vest. Except really, it's more accurate to call them bullet-*resistant* vests, because I've got some bad news for you. Body armor comes in levels. The soft vests commonly used by law enforcement won't stop any normally powered rifle bullets. To defeat a rifle bullet, you need ballistic plates, which are much bulkier and heavier, more like what you would see a soldier or SWAT team wearing.

Basically anything will go through a soft vest if it is narrow, pointy, hard, and going fast enough. There are some pistol rounds designed specifically with that kind of penetration in mind, but they're fairly unpopular. Remember that bit about the wider hole being more likely to hit something vital that will bleed more? These are the opposite of that, hitting more like an ice pick.

The sad thing about the media craze over "cop killer" bullets is that we then had cops dying because the bad guys aimed for the head instead of their body, because they were now aware the cops would likely be wearing vests. Well done, you vapid hacks.

Every now and then a politician or celebrity will go off on a tear about the latest super-ultra-deadly bullet that needs to be banned, usually while describing its ballistic performance in ways that break the laws of physics. These are always painful to listen to for anyone with even a cursory knowledge of ballistics.

On that note, you can take writing advice from Stephen King, but his opinions on guns are shockingly ignorant. (Well, actually I'd hesitate to take writing advice from him too, because that man can't write a satisfying ending to save his life.)

"We Should Ban Magazines over X Number of Shots!"

I've seen this one pop up a lot. We've done it federally before, and Congress just voted to do it again. Several states have bans on magazines holding more than some arbitrary capacity, usually ten rounds. It sounds good to the ear and really satisfies that whole "we've got to do something" need. It seems simple. Bad guys shoot a lot of people during a rampage, so if they have magazines that hold fewer rounds, ergo then they won't be able to shoot as many people.

Wrong. And I'll break it down: first, why regular folks want more rounds in our guns; second, why tactically allowing fewer rounds doesn't really stop the problem; and third, why banning magazines is a logistical impossibility.

First off, why do gun owners want magazines that hold more rounds? Because sometimes you miss. Because usually—contrary to the movies—you have to hit an opponent multiple times in order to make him stop. Because sometimes you may have multiple assailants. We don't have more rounds in the magazine so we can shoot more, we have more rounds in the magazine so we are forced to manipulate our gun less if we have to shoot more.

The 1994 Assault Weapons Ban capped capacities at ten rounds. You quickly realize ten rounds sucks when you take a wound ballistics class and go over case after case after case after case of enraged, drug-addled, prison-hardened perpetrators who soaked up five, seven, nine, even fifteen bullets and still walked to the ambulance under their own power. That isn't that uncommon. Legally, you can shoot them until they cease to be a threat; and keep in mind that what normally causes a person to stop is a loss of blood pressure, so I used to tell my students that anybody worth shooting once was worth shooting five or seven times. You shoot the attacker until he leaves you alone.

Also, you're going to miss. It is going to happen. Even if you can shoot pretty little groups at the range, those groups are going to expand dramatically under the stress and adrenaline of an actual confrontation. The more you train, the better you will perform, but you may still miss, or the bad guy might end up hiding behind something that your bullets don't penetrate. Nobody has ever survived a gunfight and then said afterwards, "Darn, I wish I hadn't brought all that extra ammo."

There's a very foolish meme that pops up whenever mag bans are proposed. It's something along the line of "shotguns are plugged to only hold three shells, so ducks have more protection than our kids." That's so dumb it makes my eye twitch. That's a law that applies when hunting birds. Do you seriously think a psychopath who is *hunting people* is going to care? *Oh no. I was about to commit murder, but I'd get a fine from a game warden.*

Our illustrious president likes to mumble something about deer don't wear Kevlar, man, and anybody who needs thirty rounds for hunting is a terrible hunter.[11] That's some patronizing gibberish. The only reason I bring it up is to demonstrate just how profoundly disingenuous one side of this debate is. This is especially galling after a year of watching mobs riot and burn cities while the police departments there told the citizens that they were on their own. Good luck.

So having more rounds in the gun is useful for self-defense. Period. And that's not even getting into the real-purpose-of-the-Second-Amendment aspects.

Now tactically, let's say a mass killer is on a rampage in a school. Unless his brain has turned to mush and he's a complete moron, he's not going to walk up to you while he reloads anyway. He's on the offense, unlike the CCW holder who gets attacked and must defend himself in whatever crappy situation he finds himself in at that time. The attacker is the aggressor. He's picked the engagement range. These are cowards who are murdering children who are running and hiding, but don't for a second make the mistake of thinking they are dumb. Many of these scumbags are actually very intelligent. They're just broken and evil.

In the cases that I'm aware of where the shooters had guns that held fewer rounds, they positioned themselves back a bit while firing, or they brought more guns and simply switched guns and kept on shooting and then reloaded before they moved to their next planned firing position. Unless you are a fumble-fingered idiot, anybody who practices in front of a mirror a few dozen times can get to where he can insert a new magazine into a gun in a few seconds.

A friend of mine, who happens to be a reasonable Democrat, was very hung up on this, certain that he would be able to take advantage of the time it took for the bad guy to reload his gun. That's a bad assumption and a whole lot of wishful thinking. This has gotten tested in force-on-force training scenarios a lot, and it usually results in the guy running in the shooter's direction getting plugged next. So that's awesome if the scenario goes down like it does in your imagination, and you can tackle him before he reloads, but good luck with that. It takes a lot less effort to just shoot him with your own gun...if you happen to be somewhere the government will let you carry one, of course.

Finally, let's look at the logistical ramifications of another magazine ban and why magazines aren't going anywhere. The AWB of '94 banned the production of all magazines over ten rounds except those marked for military or law enforcement use, and it was a felony to possess those.

Over the ten years of the ban, we never ran out. Not even close. Magazines are cheap and basic. Back then most of them were pieces of sheet metal with some wire. Now they're plastic and some wire. That's it. Magazines are considered disposable, so most gun owners accumulate a ton of them. All the AWB did was make magazines more expensive and tick off law-abiding citizens, without so much as inconveniencing a single criminal.

Because bad guys didn't run out either. And if they did, like I said, magazines are cheap and basic, so you just get or make more. If you can cook meth, you can make a functioning magazine. My gun store once designed a magazine for a niche oddball rifle, and none of us were engineers. I paid a CAD guy, spent some money, and churned out thousands of twenty-round Saiga .308 mags. This operation could've been done out of my garage. And this was long before 3D printing came along and changed everything. Now anybody can make a magazine at home using files that are everywhere. I'm not a 3D printer guy, but I'm told that once you get the bugs worked out, you can print functional Glock mag bodies for under a buck a pop.

Ten years. No difference. Meanwhile, we had bad guys turning up all the time committing crimes, and guess what was marked on the mags found in their guns? MILITARY AND LAW ENFORCE-MENT USE ONLY. Because once again, if you're already breaking a bunch of laws, they can only hang you once. Criminals simply don't care.

Just before the AWB timed out, every politician involved in possibly extending it looked at the mess that had been passed in the heat of the moment—the fact that it did nothing—and realized that every single politician from a red or purple state would lose his job if he voted for a new version. The law expired and wasn't renewed. Immediately every single gun person in America went out and bought a couple guns with Evil Features that had been previously banned and a bucket of new magazines for everything we owned, because nothing makes an American want to do something more than telling him he can't. Having learned our lesson last time, we've been stocking up ever since. If the last ban did literally nothing at all over a decade, and since then we've purchased another couple billion mags (I honestly don't know if anybody knows the actual number, but it is astronomically high), another ban will do even less...except make the law-abiding citizens even angrier, of course.

I bought forty-two more AR-15 magazines last week. I didn't need them. I've already got shelves full for my rifles. I just bought them on principle because Congress said I shouldn't have them. Trust me, I'm not alone in this practice. Gun and magazine sales skyrocket every time a politician starts to vulture in on a tragedy. When I owned my gun store, we had a picture of Barack Obama on the wall and a caption beneath it that read SALESMAN OF THE YEAR. Gun sales have blown *way* past those levels since.

So even if you could ban magazines, it wouldn't actually do anything to the crimes you want to stop. Mags are going to be in circulation. That is, unless you think you can confiscate them all, but that's a whole big apocalyptic nightmare beyond all comprehension that we'll get to in greater detail later.

"We Should Mandate 'Smart Guns'/Microstamping/Ballistic Databases (or Other Technologies That Don't Work or Don't Exist Yet)!"

Yeah, this one is pretty self-explanatory. It is silly to suggest that the only way you can exercise your rights is if you do it in a way that doesn't actually exist or work.

"Smart guns" is one of those ideas that gets proposed by some dumb state legislator every couple years. Theoretically this is a gun that couldn't be stolen by an unauthorized user because it had some kind of biometric scanner so only the rightful owner could fire it.

Have you ever tried to unlock your phone and it took a couple tries to read your fingerprint, or it froze up or took a few seconds to unlock? This is like that, except you die horribly. When you need a gun, you absolutely need it to work. Note that every single time some state proposes this, its law enforcement agencies are always exempted. That's because they're not stupid enough to trust their own safety to an easily befuddled electronic gizmo that probably won't work if their hands are sweaty. Maybe someday this technology will be reliable enough to work for self-defense use, but even then it should be a personal choice as to whether someone wants to trust it or not.

Microstamping is another technological solution that sounds great in theory but is dumb in practice. The idea is that when the gun fires, it stamps a serial number onto the shell casing, that way the casing could be matched to the weapon that fired it. That requires a registry, which gets its own section for all its problems and shortcomings, but realistically, the vast majority of the time, that serial number would just trace back to a gun that was stolen in a burglary. Not that criminals register their illegally procured guns anyway, but if they actually wanted to keep that murder weapon around for sentimental reasons, they could always just hit the microstamping part with a file beforehand.

Then there's ballistic fingerprinting, which also requires a registry. This is when manufacturers provide local authorities with a fired casing from each gun they make. In theory the casing could be used by a crime lab to match it up with the microscopic markings from any shell casings left at a crime scene. In actual practice jurisdictions that have tried this have paid large amounts of money with nothing to show for it. Maryland scrapped their ballistic fingerprinting program after spending millions on it for fifteen years and solving almost no crimes that way.[12]

What actually happens, if they can match it—heat and friction causes the "print" to change over time—is that they'll track it back to when it got reported stolen anyway. Also this does nothing for mass killers, because they're on a one-way trip, and they're going to die or surrender at the scene with their weapons, so it's not like you need to track them down. So you are basically spending a whole lot of money in order to catch that small subset of criminals who are dumb enough to commit murders with guns they purchased directly from a dealer in their own name.

Less than 2 percent of criminals buy their guns from a store. Most of them are bought from other criminals, and those were usually stolen from their rightful owners.[13]

"We Need Background Checks!"

We already have background checks for all firearms sold through federally licensed firearms dealers (or FFLs, which stands for Federal Firearms License). This basically means that if you buy a gun from a gun store, you have to fill out paperwork (the 4473 form), present ID, and then the FFL calls it in to the National Instant Criminal Background Check System (NICS). In some cases your state will have its own background system instead of the federal one. Either way, they are looking at the purchaser's records to see if he is a "prohibited person" for whatever reason. That's anything that would prevent you from possessing a firearm legally, like being a convicted felon, being under felony indictment, having been dishonorably discharged from the military, renouncing your citizenship, having a domestic violence restraining order against you, or that sort of thing.

If the check comes back clean and you're not a prohibited person, you can now purchase the gun.

There's this weird misconception that because the check is instant, it is less thorough. The amount of time to process it makes no difference. It's computerized. You are either marked as a prohibited person or you are not. It's not like if the background check takes days they're actually going out and investigating you again. Now, the state doing a terrible job at updating its own records, with the result that people should be marked as prohibited but aren't, does happen. No amount of demanding stricter background checks is going to magically make the government more competent at filling out its own paperwork.

Background checks are one of those things that sound appealing on paper, but in reality they're pretty much useless.

Say you are a prohibited person, but you want to do some crime. You need a piece. You've got a record, so you can't just buy a gun at a store—so what do you do? Well, most of the time you're just going to steal one or buy one on the street that's been stolen by somebody else. But let's say you're feeling really particular, and there's something new and specific you want to buy from an FFL. That's what straw purchases are for.

A straw purchase is when a prohibited person gets someone who can pass a background check to buy the gun for him. This is already illegal.

Usually it works like this. I'm working at the gun counter of your friendly neighborhood gun monger. A young man walks in and starts looking at the handguns in the glass case, until he keys in on one. I ask if I can help him. "Nah, man, I'm good," he replies. Then he leaves. Two minutes later a young woman walks in and wants to buy that exact same gun, even though she clearly has no idea what she's doing. So basically the dude went out to his car, told his girlfriend, "Go get me that one," and now she's going to commit a felony for him. And it is often that painfully obvious because many of these guys aren't exactly brain surgeons.

When an FFL suspects it's a straw purchase, we don't do the sale, and we report the attempt. I've seen people make the stupid claim that, no, dealers wouldn't care, that we'd just look the other way and take the money. Whoever believes that has never dealt with the ATF—an agency known for its tendency to shoot your dog and burn your house down—because there's a very good chance that obvious straw purchaser was sent by the ATF to test you. They do that. Any FFL dumb enough to engage in transactions like that is too dumb to stay in business.

However, if the prohibited person isn't a totally obvious idiot about it, and your straw purchaser plays it cool and just acts like a regular customer, he (or she) would be nearly impossible to notice, thus thwarting the background check system. Not that this matters anyway, because even though it is already a felony to lie on your 4473 form—I'm looking at you, Hunter Biden[14]—and it is illegal to attempt a straw purchase, these violations are almost never followed up on by law enforcement.

When Barack Obama's pick to head the ATF testified before a Senate committee, he acknowledged that of 48,321 cases involving attempted straw purchases, the Justice Department had prosecuted a whopping forty-four of them.[15]

I was unable to find more recent data, but I'd assume this ratio hasn't changed that significantly. Keep in mind there are *millions* of background checks performed every month, so that is a lot of effort being expended to prosecute a handful of clumsy crooks.

Yet in order to make our background check system work, FFLs are required to keep meticulous records in what is called a "bound book." That's where all guns are tracked by serial number as they are transferred in and then matched to a 4473 when they go out. The same government that makes massive mistakes all the time on people's background data will smite the living hell out of an FFL who makes a clerical error on their paperwork.

Then there's the occasional screw up, where somebody who is not a prohibited person gets flagged by the system incorrectly, can't buy a gun, and has to jump through a bunch of hoops to clear his name. And when I say name, I'm being literal, because that's usually what I saw when an unfortunate law-abiding citizen had a name that was the same or really close to that of somebody with a criminal record.

There have been a few high-profile mass killings recently where the bad guy purchased his gun from a store and passed the background check—obviously, if they've got no criminal history, there is nothing to flag. They're going to pass. It's a background check. Not a secret-evil-plot detector.

So the state has mandated an expensive system that requires regular people to be inconvenienced and dealers to spend money, time, and effort—and the state doesn't bother to investigate the system or prosecute the vast majority of the violations anyway.

It's almost as if getting the *Do-Something* was more important than the actual results.

"We Need to Close the Gun Show Loophole!"

I'd bet nine times out of ten when I hear this one the speaker has absolutely no idea what it even means. Gun shows are like a swap meet/farmer's market for guns, though there are often more beef jerky and T-shirt vendors than firearms, depending on how good your local shows are. People seem to think that if you buy a gun at a show there's no requirement for a background check, except that's not how it works.

This Do-Something is actually a continuation of the last one about background checks.

FFLs are *always* required to fill out a 4473 and perform a background check when selling guns to people. It doesn't matter if they are at their store or at a gun show. The location is irrelevant. Most of the actual tables and booths at gun shows are FFLs (well, not the beef jerky ones, obviously).

The "loophole" they're talking about is private citizens selling their private property. These are regular people who are not gun dealers, who want to sell a gun they own to another regular person. This is stuff like, "I bought this Beretta, but it is really expensive, and now I can't pay rent, so I'm going to sell it." Or, "Grandpa died, he left some old shotguns in the closet; I don't shoot, and I need the money." Or, "Even though I bought this gun, it turned out to be an inaccurate and unreliable piece of crap, so now I want to get rid of it—to somebody who doesn't care but thinks it is pretty" (not naming any brands!).

They call this the "gun show loophole," because gun shows are places people congregate to buy and sell guns; so obviously if you want to sell something, you go to where people are specifically buying. However, this could be anywhere. You could sell a gun to your neighbor. Bob from accounting stuck a notice on the company bulletin board saying he wants to sell this Smith & Wesson 629, and you picked it up in the parking lot and then bought him lunch. That sort of thing.

Now, if you are routinely buying and selling guns to turn a profit, the ATF will declare that you are engaging in business and should be an FFL. So this is very specifically targeted at regular people.

American citizens owning property isn't a "loophole."

Closing the gun show loophole basically means forcing regular Americans to jump through all the same hoops, and do all the same paperwork, as a professional federally licensed firearms dealer who is trained and does it for a living. Trust me, that sucks. Remember when I talked about keeping a "bound book" of meticulous records? To make this actually work, regular people would have to do something equivalent to that.

And I forgot to mention the part where FFLs get randomly audited by the ATF, where their bound book is inspected and matched to every physical serial number on the premises and every 4473 for every serial number that has left. It's super fun, and if my sarcasm isn't coming through, it's like getting a colonoscopy. But how else will the government know if regular people have been processing proper background checks for whatever private property they decide to sell?

The other possibility is requiring regular citizens to only be able to transfer their private property through an FFL. Which is basically a federally mandated middleman, adding cost, time, and hassle, because FFLs aren't going to volunteer to get extra colonoscopies for free.

That's a lot of extra work to force people into a background check that criminals easily circumvent. The government doesn't even bother to prosecute the dumb ones who get caught violating it anyway.

"You Keep Saying Criminals Steal Guns, So We Should Mandate Safe Storage Laws So Guns Don't Fall into the Wrong Hands!"

Which is basically you declaring that only well-off homeowners have a right to keep and bear arms. Actual serious-duty gun safes that will deter a burglar are very expensive, and you're probably not bolting one of those heavy things to the floor of a rental. And even though a safe will slow a random crackhead, if you're dealing with an actual thief, he's bringing real tools to defeat it.

Don't get me wrong, I am a firm believer that all responsible gun owners should store their guns in a way that's secure as possible and out of the reach of unauthorized users. However, I think the state mandating how to secure your property is dumb, because the government will always come up with a one-size-fits-all solution that checks boxes but doesn't actually work well for any individual's particular needs. We all have different circumstances, and what works for me with older kids who are all trained shooters in a big house way out in the country might not work for someone with younger children in an apartment in the city, and so forth. You want to keep your defensive guns in a way that they are inaccessible to anyone you don't want messing with them, but accessible to you when you need them so you can still access them quickly and efficiently.

Some states require certain kinds of firearms storage. These laws are inevitably stupider than what a trained individual would decide was best for their situation. The Supreme Court decision in *District of Columbia v. Heller* in 2008 shot down D.C.'s requirement that guns be kept unloaded, disassembled, or locked.

"Child safety locks" are just plain idiotic and exist because some bureaucrat thought that was a brilliant idea. It is mandatory that they come included with all new pistols, but as soon as gun owners get the box with the new gun home, that cheap cable lock that comes with it gets tossed in the trash. These locks are utterly useless for defensive firearms. When you need a weapon, you need it right away. You're not going to find a key, unlock a cable lock, free it from the action, load the gun and... oh wait, you got murdered somewhere around step two. Never mind.

"We Have to Ban Ghost Guns!"

Now this one takes the cake for scariest-sounding nonsense buzz word. Homemade gun doesn't sound nearly as impressive. "Ghost gun" sounds pretty badass and dangerous, but it just means it's a gun without a serial number.

Ah-ha! The anti-gunner shrieks, no serial number clearly means that this is meant to be an untraceable crime gun for movie-style hitmen.

Not really. Only guns that are built by licensed manufacturers and sold through FFLs require serial numbers. If you build a gun yourself for personal use, there's no serial number required. That's it. That's the big freak-out about ghost guns.

Americans have been building guns at home since we were a British colony. If you are mechanically inclined, it's actually a pretty fun hobby. As tools got better and things like drill presses became cheaper, home builds became more common. With 3D printing, home building went absolutely nuts, and there are communities of inventive gun nuts open-sourcing files for each other to experiment on and improve. This is all perfectly legal.

Some manufacturers sell kits that have parts and blocks for the end-user hobbyist to machine and assemble themselves. For things like that, the ATF has some bizarre and arbitrary rules about how finished they can be before they are considered a firearm. Basically with modern technology, even if you are starting from scratch with bare blocks of metal, firearms just aren't that complicated to make.

Any idiot can make a rudimentary gun. With a bit of skill and some resources, you can make a pretty effective weapon. If you've got some mechanical skill, access to an actual shop, and good equipment, you can build pretty much whatever you want. Regardless of whether it was built at home or bought from a store, it's still just a gun, and we've already gone over why each type of those should be legal.

Supposedly criminals love ghost guns because they are untraceable and can be procured without a background check—except we already went over how much criminals care about background checks: not at all. As far as tracing the serial number of a gun found at a crime scene, it's usually going to get traced back to a burglary where some other crook stole it from a law-abiding citizen's home or vehicle.

Will some criminals build their own guns? Sure. Like I said, it's not hard. We live in a world where drug cartels have their own submarines, and you think bad guys aren't going to get guns if they want them? We made buying cold medicine a pain in the ass to try and stop people from cooking meth, and that seems to be working splendidly, that is, more meth than ever.

My personal thought on this one is that the harder authoritarians push for gun control, the more the home-build community grows. They can't really ban *knowledge*. I think the very concept of gun bans has been destroyed forever by technology, and the anti-gunners just don't realize it yet. Even if a magical genie granted their wish and made all their wildest gun control dreams come true, all the existing guns vanished, and all the manufacturers were sued out of existence, the next day enterprising home builders would print more.

In Myanmar, 3D printed guns are showing up in guerilla warfare now, made entirely out of innocuous parts that can't be regulated, and Americans have a lot more resources to work with.[16]

There is no banning ghost guns. They're the guns that will always exist specifically because control freaks keep talking about banning stuff. They should have called them "spite guns." That name would be more accurate.

"There Should Be a Waiting Period before You Can Buy a Gun to Prevent Crimes of Passion!"

Okay, you convinced me. I will reach across the aisle in the spirit of bipartisanship and compromise on this one and allow for a seventy-two-hour "cooling off" period before you can take home any atomic bombs.

Seriously though, this is one of the dumbest and most offensive of all of these Do-Somethings.

So citizens can pass a background check, but they still have to wait some arbitrary amount of time before they exercise their rights? That's foolishness. And it has already been tried in various jurisdictions where it has been shown to be totally pointless.

If it is an actual "crime of passion" and they can't get a gun from one of the many illegal sources—or they are cool with murder but draw the line at stealing—why wouldn't they just use one of the multitudes of other convenient murder weapons mankind has been using for thousands of years? I mean, if you're really feeling passionately murdery, Cain bashed Abel with a rock. Alternatively, they could just wait the three-to-ten business days or whatever it is in that state and use that time to plan, and buy supplies like tarps, shovels, and bleach to do a proper premeditated crime that they'll be a lot more likely to get away with.

Waiting periods are naïve wishful thinking in the hopes that somebody who really wants to commit murder will experience a miraculous "Come to Jesus" moment during that arbitrary time window and decide to turn his life around. Instead, what actually happens is that regular people who procrastinated purchasing a firearm suddenly find themselves in need of one, but can't get one. Or they were politically opposed to owning a gun. Then something horrible happens, reality kicks their philosophy in the junk, and they need something to defend themselves with. Now.

Oh wait. You can't. Good luck! Try not to die!

With this one I'm specifically talking about liberal Californians, who never wanted an icky gun in their house…until rioting engulfed their neighborhood, the local police retreated, and suddenly that Second Amendment thing starts to sound real appealing. Only then they find out their state government makes them wait ten days before they can bring home a gun. In that case the "cooling off" period refers to the ashes after their homes or businesses get burned down.

It is wise for people to get armed and trained in advance of a crisis, but procrastination shouldn't be a barrier to exercising your constitutional rights.

This Do-Something is so dumb that I doubt any of its advocates actually believe it works. It's really more revenge against people who disagree with them politically. The process is the punishment.

"I'm Offended by All This Gun Talk. Red Flag! Red Flag!"

Alright, that's not how red flag laws usually get pitched, but you get the idea.

In theory red flag laws—officially known as Extreme Risk Protective Orders (ERPO)—are supposed to be used by regular honest people to alert law enforcement that somebody they know is planning something dangerous, so the cops can swoop in and take away all his guns. That way once he is disarmed he can't do whatever bad thing he was planning anymore.

Uh-huh...Because as we all know laws are only ever used in the most ideal way possible.

This is also one of the Do-Somethings that enjoys bipartisan support, as we've seen recently with fourteen Republican senators agreeing with all the Democrats to pass a bill that would fund red flag laws in all fifty states. The details of how this is all supposed to work are going to vary from state to state. Currently nineteen states and the District of Columbia have ERPOs, with most of those being put into place over the last few years, but that number will certainly rise dramatically after the passage of this latest bill.[17]

They make the idealized pitch sound kind of nice and appealing. That weird teenager from down the street, you know the one who likes to torture small animals? Yeah, that kook. It turns out his Instagram is all maps of his school and pictures of other kids in his yearbook with their faces cut out labeled "To-Do List" and photos of his guns titled "Murder trial exhibit 1." Let's helpfully alert the police.

Then the police swoop in, take the weirdo's guns, and after being properly chastised, he will turn into a productive member of society. Yay.

What we're actually worried about is more like this. You know that guy, Bob, who disagreed with me at the HOA meeting once and has those campaign signs in his yard for politicians I don't like? He posted a picture of a disgusting, icky assault rifle with a "shoulder thing that goes up" on his Instagram, and he was shooting it with his children. Gross. I'm disgusted and afraid, so I'm going to alert the police about this madman's evil plots.

Then the police swoop in, take the weirdo's guns without any of that pesky due process, and then after several years of fighting with the state and paying large sums of money for lawyers, Bob might get his expensive property back. That's assuming of course that the cops didn't just shoot Bob in the face when they no-knock raided his house at 3:00 a.m. to seize his guns.

Ironically, the Venn diagram of people who love the idea of red flag laws and people who protested the Breonna Taylor shooting that happened during a police raid pretty much make a circle.

You might think that my hypothetical scenario is far-fetched. It's not. We live in a "Karen demands to speak to your manager" world. There are legions of axe grinders, jerks, disgruntled employees, angry ex-wives, and people who call 911 because they saw a black dude walking down the sidewalk suspiciously. These are the same kind of people who get offended by something you said, then go through reporting all your posts on social media hoping you'll get banned. This is like that, only it enables them to legally send a SWAT team to your house to take your property and kill you if you resist.

ERPOs are ripe for abuse, and even though these laws have only been in a few states for more than a handful of years, we've already seen crap like this happen. The most infamous early one was a woman in Colorado red-flagging a police officer who had shot her son—even though the shooting had been in the line of duty, was a really obvious suicide by cop, and had been ruled justified. This one was so blatantly absurd it eventually got tossed by a judge, but it is an example that grudge holders will weaponize the law for revenge.[18]

The question isn't if red flags will be abused, but by how much. That will depend on how the state laws are written. I'd love to see huge fines and jail time put in place to dissuade awfuls from using

ERPOs like a hammer to bludgeon whomever they don't like with BS claims, but I won't hold my breath.

We've established that neighbor Bob is going to get screwed over by Karen, but what about Johnny School-Shooter? Maybe red flag laws will stop some maniacs from going on a rampage? The actual statistical data on ERPOs making a difference is totally inconclusive, and always will be.[19] Mass killings make headlines and get all the lurid coverage, but they don't happen that often. However, think through the repercussions.

Say bag-of-dead-cats guy gets red-flagged. Let's assume he really was planning on going on a killing spree. He gets reported, the cops come take his guns...Now what? That'll depend on the state laws, most of which aren't written yet. Do they just leave him there? Sure, he's unarmed—for now. Briefly. Until he procures another gun from one of the multitude of sources that supply the vast majority of guns actually used in crimes in this country. Or he switches tactics and just builds a bomb with supplies from Home Depot or uses his truck to drive through a parade instead.

Alternately, our outcast *is* a disgruntled, angry, disaffected ass-hole, but he was *not* actually planning any killing sprees. Until he got an ERPO served on him at least. Now he feels like a hated pariah who has been labeled a menace to society even though he hadn't actually done anything wrong. Then after the cops leave him, temporarily disarmed but stewing in rage, I'm sure he'll learn from this and become a much kinder, gentler, and less-inclined-to-murder sort of person.

There are many different kinds of killers. We have many examples of murderers being known to law enforcement well in advance of their killing anyone. Some of these had criminal records a mile long, so they were already legally prohibited from owning a gun at all, and thus officially "disarmed," but then they got a gun anyway. Other killers would never draw any red flags at all. They were the proverbial "he was a quiet man, really kept to himself, never bothered nobody"— until he did.

The type of killer that well-meaning red flag advocates are imagining will be stopped by ERPOs is the kind who gives off all the warning signs in the world. They're threatening, crazy, do violent things, hurt the people around them, et cetera. They are clearly a danger to themselves and others. They're psychos, and everybody knows it and warns their friends to avoid them. They're ticking time bombs.

Except there are already involuntary commitment standards for people like that. Only states rarely use them, and when they do, it is usually based on some standard of them being *imminently* dangerous, as in they are about to do something bad *right now*. If everyone figures they are dangerous, but they're not actively on their way to blow something up, the state can't be bothered. Dealing with that is expensive and legally messy.

Many mass killers were known to law enforcement in advance, sometimes with dozens of tips to local police and the FBI, and nothing was done. Meanwhile, we've got combat vets who refuse to seek out professional help for their PTSD because they're afraid that diagnoses will be used as an excuse for the state to strip them of their rights. And after looking at this giant list of Do-Somethings, can you blame them for being worried? Red flag laws are a dream come true for authoritarians.

Recently there were high-profile mass murders in New York and Illinois. In both cases the attackers were known in advance to law enforcement and had given off a multitude of warning signs long before they went on their rampages. New York and Illinois both have red flag laws.[20]

All gun laws are supposed to stop criminals, but instead end up hassling law-abiding citizens. This is inevitable because dealing with criminals is hard while abusing law-abiding citizens is easy. I see no reason to think that red flag laws will end up being any different.

Chapter Five

Do Something Even Harder!

"We Should Just Ban All the Guns Then. You Only Need Them to Murder People Anyway! The Social Cost Is Too High!"

It doesn't really make sense to ban guns, because in reality what that means is that you are actually trying to ban effective self-defense. Despite the constant hammering by a news media with an agenda, guns are used in America far more often to stop crime than to cause crime.

I've seen several different sets of numbers about how many times guns are used in self-defense every year. The problem with keeping track of this stat is that the vast majority of the time, when a gun is used in a legal self-defense situation, no shots are fired. The mere presence of the gun is enough to cause the criminal to stop. Notable firearms instructor Clint Smith had a saying: "If you look like food, you will be eaten." Regular criminals are looking for prey. They want easy victims. If they wanted to work hard for a living, they'd get a job.

When you pull a gun, you are no longer prey, you are work, so they're usually going to go find somebody easier to pick on.

Many defensive gun uses (DGUs) never get tracked as such. From personal experience, I have pulled a gun on another human being one time in my entire life. I was legally justified, and the aggressor stopped, lowered his gun, and left. My one defensive gun use was never recorded as a stat anywhere as far as I know, because no shots were fired.

My wife has used a firearm in self-defense twice in her life. Once on somebody who was acting very rapey, who suddenly found a better place to be when she stuck a pistol in his face, and again years later on a German Shepherd that was attacking my one-year-old son. No police report at all on the second one, and I don't believe the first one ever turned up as any sort of defensive use statistic because no shots were fired.

So how often are guns used in self-defense?

One of the most commonly cited studies estimates that there are around 2.5 million defensive gun uses a year, which is orders of magnitude higher than our number of murders.[1]

America's murder rate had been trending steadily downward over the last two decades, until in 2020 it skyrocketed to the highest number it's been in twenty-five years, with over 21,000 murders.[2] Keep in mind not all of those murders were done with firearms. Twenty nineteen is the last year I could find a detailed breakdown from the FBI, which is showing 13,927 murders, with approximately 74 percent (10,258) of those being done with guns.[3]

Why was there such an astoundingly *massive* increase in homicides in 2020? What current events could have possibly influenced that number? This was the year of "fiery but mostly peaceful" protests, and people chanting "All Cops Are Bastards," while cities let hoodlums start up their own "autonomous zones." Big city DAs decided to quit sending violent criminals to jail. Grifters changed Black Lives Matter to Buy Large Mansions,[4] and the very people they were supposedly helping had their neighborhoods engulfed in violence and chaos for it. It's almost like letting criminals do whatever they want, unimpeded by the law, Mad Max–dystopia-style has negative consequences or something.

Regardless, that still puts defensive gun uses about 119 times higher than even our crappiest murder year of recent times.

But to really drive this home, let's not go with the high estimate. Let's go with some smaller ones instead. Since everybody who takes a crack at this sets different parameters for their studies, results vary wildly, with papers citing numbers between 500,000 and 3 million defensive gun uses a year.[5]

Let's use that far more conservative 500,000 number. That still absolutely dominates that homicide number. In fact, the absolute lowest estimated number I could find anywhere was 100,000, which is kind of absurd once you hear that the average result of seventeen other surveys was 2 million.[6]

The only kind of people dishonest enough to try and sell that 100K number are the vultures. Yet even given that ludicrously low estimate, the good guys still win by a rather substantial margin. So even if you use the worst number provided by people who are just as biased as I am, but in the opposite direction, defensive gun use is a huge net positive. Or to put it another way, anti-gun zealots hate your owning guns so much that they are totally cool with the population of a fairly large city getting assaulted, raped, and murdered every year as collateral damage in order to get what they want.

The thing to remember about vulture statistics is that they're always twisted for emotional impact. Mark Twain talked about lies, damned lies, and statistics, but our modern anti-gun zealots would have blown his mind. Their goal is to toss out something that sounds lurid and ghastly, truth be damned, and by the time it is debunked it doesn't matter, because liars and useful idiots will just regurgitate it forever. Like the infamous *a gun in the home is forty-three times more likely to kill you or a loved one than an intruder.* That one is straight up nonsense, created with embarrassingly flawed methods, from a tiny sample, that even the author has since revised down to a tiny fraction of that (and he's still grasping at straws to get there), yet they've been unabashedly repeating this thoroughly debunked lie since 1986.[7] I was in sixth grade. Original *Top Gun* was in theaters. They've got no shame!

Back to comparing the social costs, I've been talking about homicides versus DGUs, but what about criminals using firearms in crimes that don't result in homicides? That's an even harder number to pin down. What are the parameters used to define that? Like they actually shot at somebody? Or they had one on them while performing some other kind of crime? In searching for this, I found a lot fewer options to choose from. One of the few estimates I could find was from the National Crime Victimization Study, at 480,000.[8]

Comparing that to the average estimate, DGU's win handily; compared to the really low estimate, they come out about even—and I doubt anybody who has read this far is gullible enough to buy NPR's goofy partisan number.[9]

When it comes down to these debates about "social costs," one of the manipulative things that anti-gun zealots like to do is lump suicides in with murders and then call them "gun deaths" or "gun violence," usually while leaving out that over half of that number in any given year are suicides. People see the dramatically larger number and just assume those are all murders rather than someone punching their own ticket.

This is sleazy, disingenuous, and also ignores the fact that the methods of suicide are interchangeable. There are countries with far higher suicide rates than us, where civilian gun ownership is exceedingly rare or almost impossible.[10] Americans use guns because they are common tools here. A lack of tools doesn't stop people in other countries from committing suicide, where they use hanging, knives, or stepping off tall buildings instead.

This one especially galls me. Suicide is a serious issue, and anybody contemplating it should seek help immediately. It's not about the tool used, it's about dealing with whatever heartache brought them to that point.

The vultures also like to lump in things like justified homicides, good guys shooting bad guys, and cops shooting criminals to inflate their numbers.[11] Zealots don't care if its murder or suicide, justified or illegal, every death is just a stat to milk for political gain.

Regardless of how much they pump up the terror, we've established that guns are overwhelmingly beneficial for self-defense purposes.

Embrace the fact that we are tool-using mammals.

"Why Don't You Just Use Something other than a Stupid Gun? I Saw an Ad for (Insert Less Effective Self-Defense Gizmo Here)."

There are other methods of self-defense, but none of them are the great equalizer. I am a huge fan of having different tools in your toolbox. I carry pepper spray. I don't leave home without my spicy-treat dispenser. However, I recognize that it isn't always effective and isn't the best answer in some circumstances. I've studied martial arts, and I'm a big strong guy who enjoys fighting. I've taken classes that spend a lot of time teaching you all the best ways to manage unknown contacts, avoid threats, deescalate conflict, and how to survive when you can't. Despite all that I absolutely still carry a concealed handgun everywhere I can.

Like the great philosopher Harry Callahan said, "A man's got to know his limitations."[12] Even big, strong men can get their skulls caved in, and no matter how much you can bench, it doesn't make you bulletproof. No matter how tough or skilled you may be, there are some situations where a gun is simply your most effective response. Even if you are a certified badass, you probably can't jujitsu your way out of a shooting. Most of the hardcore MMA guys I know carry guns too. This isn't an attitude thing. It's not compensating. It's just simple physics.

Now take people who may be smaller, weaker, younger, older, infirm, or disabled. What are they supposed to do against a violent, determined aggressor? You pepper sprayed him. You used your junior college women's self-defense class moves. It didn't work. He's still trying to hurt you. You've got no escape. Now what? Wait for the police to save you? I sure hope you don't live within the Uvalde city limits.

We've all seen internet or Hollywood tough guys posture about how nobody needs guns because if there was trouble, they'd just handle their business with their bare hands...Great. Sure you would, bro. Now let's do your same imaginary situation, but instead of you, it's your mom. Or your grandma. Plus, let's be honest, we all know those types are full of crap or downright delusional, and in the case of the movie stars, they'd just have their armed security guards take care of the problem for them.

There are times when you simply need a gun, or you're gonna die.

If you believe human beings have a right to defend themselves, then by logical extension you should believe in the right to keep and bear arms. If you want everyone disarmed, then you don't really believe in the right of self-defense, and you're okay with other people dying in order to placate your angst or punish your political foes. It is that simple.

"Boo Evil Gun Culture!"

Or insert any of the other traditional accusations here instead. We're a bunch of bloodthirsty rednecks who just want to shoot people, or some nonsense about sexual compensation, or how we love our guns more than children, or whatever other emotionally manipulative, thought-terminating cliches the anti-gun side uses to try to shame everyone into silence.

They all boil down to the same basic premise. If you want to possess a firearm in order to defend yourself, your family, and your property, you must be morally repugnant in some way. If only we caved in to their demands, the world would magically turn into a better place where bad things no longer happen. Legal gun owners are the real villains for standing in the way.

Really? Because I hate to break it to you, when nearly eight hundred people get murdered in beautiful gun-free Chicago every year,[13] that's not my people doing the shooting.

Regular gun owners are all around you (well, except for those of you reading this in elite liberal urban city centers where you've extinguished your gun culture). We are your friends, neighbors, and coworkers.

I think the biggest reason gun control has become an increasingly difficult sell is that, as CCW has become more common, it has removed much of the stigma against regular people being armed. When I first got interested in gun rights thirty years ago, there were seventeen states that allowed concealed carry, nineteen where it was possible but extremely restricted, and fourteen with no concealed carry at all. Now it is twenty-five with no restrictions, seventeen that allow it, and eight that keep it extremely restricted—and those eight are the dinosaurs, and a recent Supreme Court decision is their extinction-causing meteor.[14]

At this point in time, everybody outside of elite urban city centers knows somebody who lawfully carries a firearm. So they're aware that these are just regular people who want to be able to defend themselves. It's become increasingly difficult to paint your dentist or your real estate agent as a trigger-happy boogeyman.

There is a demographic that often gets labeled as "the gun culture." These are the people who are adamant about the right to keep and bear arms. Contrary to how it is portrayed in the news—poorly— the gun culture is not some monolithic group that marches in lockstep, nor is it the wholly owned subsidiary of any political party or lobbying group. Like every other bunch of human beings who happen to be united on one thing, we're diverse about everything else, with different backgrounds, interests, and beliefs. We come from wildly different places. There are generational differences, cultural differences, sociological and economic differences, and so on.

It is a big tent, and it's been getting bigger.

The gun culture is who protects our country. Sure, there are plenty of soldiers and cops who are issued guns and who use them as part of their jobs who could care less. However, the people who build the guns, really understand the guns, actually enjoy using the guns, and usually end up being picked to teach everybody else how to use the guns are the gun culture.

The media and politicians would absolutely love to end the gun culture in America, because then they could finally pass all the laws they wanted to without listening to all those uppity voters. There has been an endless cultural barrage demeaning gun owners by the same media that has absolutely no problem glorifying violence, often in the same shows. Sure, the hero shoots dozens of mooks per episode, but that's cool because the writers put in something about how he's elite and special, so it's okay when he's armed. Meanwhile, us peasants are just there to be victims, and if a regular citizen uses a gun on TV, it usually just makes things worse. Then there's always that Very Special Episode where some innocent gets shot on accident and actors who barely know the bullets come out the pointy end solemnly lecture us about the need to Do Something. There are obviously exceptions to this, but overwhelmingly Hollywood is all in on the anti-gun messaging.

There was a push there for a while where doctors would ask their patients if there were any guns in their homes. That's because whenever the control freaks are losing the argument about "gun safety," they try to reframe it as a "public health issue." It isn't. But doctors are supposed to be seen as trustworthy authority figures, so the goal is just to shame you into compliance.

There's anti-gun messaging from every major institution in society. There are posters on the walls at your kid's school and your corporate job. Anti-gun marches are showered in praise, while pro-gun marches generate terror warnings, and if they do show up on the news, it's only with cherry-picked video showing the weirdest dude there while cropping out the normal respectable types. If you are a black, Asian, or Latino gun owner at any pro-gun event, the news will go to hilariously absurd lengths to crop you out of all the pictures. Every crime that's useful for their narrative gets endlessly repeated in lurid detail, while stories of regular people defending themselves rarely get covered at all, and if they do, it is on page twenty of the local newspaper.

I'll go into a lot more detail about this relentless culture war later, but basically the entire process is designed to make gun owners feel like pariahs so we'll shut up and get in line. They want us shamed out of existence so we will quit correcting their lies and voting wrong.

Let's take a look at what happens when a country finally succeeds in utterly stamping out its gun culture. Mumbai, 2008. Ten armed jihadi terrorists simply walked into town and started shooting people. It was a rather direct, straightforward, ham-fisted terrorist attack. They killed 164 people and wounded over 300. India has incredibly strict gun laws, but once again, criminals don't care.

That's not my point this time however, because I want to look at the response. These ten men terrorized a city and murdered people for four days.[15] Depending on where this happened in America, it would have been over in four minutes or four hours. The Indian police responded, but their tactics sucked. Their marksmanship sucked. Their leadership sucked. Their response utterly and completely fell apart.

Afterwards I was able to speak to some individuals from a government agency who were involved in the aftermath and investigation, all of whom are well-trained, well-practiced gun nuts. They told me the problem was that the police had no clue what to do because they'd never been taught what to do. Their leadership hated and feared the gun so much that they stamped out the ability for any of their men to actually master the tool. When you kill your gun culture, you kill off your instructors and those who can pass down the knowledge necessary to do the job.

Don't think that we're so far off here. Several years ago I was doing a book signing in one of the biggest cities in the U.S. Afterwards I went to dinner with a bunch of fans who were on the local metro PD. These guys were all SWAT or narcotics cops, all of them were gun nuts who practiced on their own dime, and each was intimately familiar with real violence. These are the guys that you want responding when the real bad stuff goes down. These were not the kind of cops who go to cower and wait in a hallway checking their emails or applying hand sanitizer during a mass killing. Each of them had been tested in real life and had run toward the sound of the guns.

What they told me made me sick. Their leadership was all uniformly liberal and extremely anti-gun, just like most big cities in America. They walked me through what their responses were supposed to be in case of a Mumbai-style event, and how their "scary assault weapons" were kept locked up where they would be unavailable. The training for their rank and file was dismal, and the city had run off or shut down all their shooting ranges, so they didn't even have places to practice anymore.

So now the cops were less safe, the city they were protecting was less safe, the bad guys were safer—the innocent bystanders in their backstop, not so much—but most importantly their leadership could pat themselves on the back, because they'd *done something*. This dinner predated Black Lives Matter, ACAB, and Defund the Police, so I can't imagine the situation has gotten better since.

"The Gun Manufacturers Should Be Held Accountable!"

For what? Having their legal product used in an illegal manner?

Despite Joe Biden's inane speeches on the subject, firearms manufacturers have civil liability like any other company. If they produce a product that is defective and it blows up in your hands, you can still sue them. What the anti-gun zealots want is an entirely different level of accountability, where the maker is responsible for whatever horrible thing the end user does with their product.

By this terrible logic, Ford Motor Company is responsible for a lunatic driving his Explorer through a parade in Waukesha. Rational people would look at that situation and say that there is no way that is Ford's fault. Ford manufactured a perfectly normal automobile, which is used responsibly and legally by millions of people every day, so of course the manufacturer should bear no responsibility for the actions of one of their customers who turned out to be an evil psychopath.

But you flip that around to guns, and disingenuous types pretend that it is totally different. Remington manufactured a perfectly normal rifle, which is used responsibly and legally by millions of people every day, but they are responsible for the actions of one of their customers who turned out to be an evil psychopath?

Both are legal, common, everyday items. Only one of them is utterly despised by one part of the political spectrum, so anything goes.

Another angle of attack is to pick a gun that was used in a crime, and then blame it on that gun's marketing. *Oh, so this ad says your rifle is accurate. Clearly that means it's accurate for shooting at children! You are trying to sell this to child shooters, aren't you, Mr. Gun Company?*

It's profoundly dishonest. Nobody is actually dumb enough to believe any of this makes sense, but this is just political lawfare, throwing suits at their opponents in the hopes of breaking them financially.

"I'd Be More Comfortable If You Gun People Were Forced to Have More Mandatory Training."

This Do-Something is usually accompanied by a tortured analogy equating gun ownership to getting a driver's license. Except mandatory training is a placebo at best. This is a subject that has caused some division amongst gun rights advocates over the years, but I'm firmly against any sort of legally mandated training for private citizens before they can exercise their rights.

To clarify, I'm a huge fan of training. I think gun school is great. I've taken many classes over the years, and I still try to take at least one or two classes annually to continue my education and not become stagnant. I think if you're going to own a gun or carry a gun, it behooves you to seek out quality instructors and keep learning.

But mandatory training, required by the state, before you are allowed to defend yourself? Absolutely not.

There have been different kinds of mandatory training required to get a CCW. When I got started, some states required attending a classroom lecture, others required classroom time and an actual shooting test. The length of the classes and the difficulty of the test varied greatly state to state. And there was one state (Vermont) that required no training or license at all, so anybody who wasn't a prohibited person could just carry a gun.[16]

When I first started teaching CCW I did a full-on basic live-fire handgun class in addition to the lecture portion required by the state. What I quickly discovered was the people who were going to be smart were smart. People who were going to be stupid were on their best behavior while I watched them, then immediately went back to being stupid when they were on their own. People who want to get trained pay attention. People who are there because it's required do the absolute minimum and then forget it as soon as they reach the parking lot. Sort of like every other kind of mandatory training for every other single field ever, in all of recorded human history. So no big surprise there.

Shooting is a skill that can be taught. Those who want to learn are going to learn. Those with giant egos assume that what they already know is good enough, and you can't teach them anything anyway. Plus, shooting is only one part of the equation, and not the most important part either. Don't get me wrong, being able to hit your target is important, but it pales in comparison to the importance of making good decisions. I can teach a monkey to hit a piece of paper. Teaching someone to react intelligently under stress is a whole lot harder.

Even mandatory training often has giant gaping holes in what it covers, and one-size-fits-all training rarely helps with an individual's specific needs. Mandatory minimum standards get you a lot of mandatory minimum instructors producing mandatory minimum shooters. This isn't just for gun stuff, but you've all seen it in whatever it is you do for a living. What boxes are we required to check? Let's hurry and check them.

The old Utah course required a bunch of extraneous stuff that was best learned on your own, or from the owner's manual, yet there was only a small section about use of force laws, when you can shoot, why you should shoot, and absolutely nothing at all about tactics.

There was no section about what to do after a shooting, how to deal with the responding officers, or what the legal aftermath would be like...but I was legally required to spend time explaining stuff like the difference between rimfire and centerfire.

After about a year, I changed up my CCW class. If a student wanted to learn to shoot better, then he could come to an actual shooting class. Then I expanded my classroom portion. I'd cover the mandatory basic silly requirements, then spend the majority of the time going over use of force, decision making, and the stuff that keeps you (a) alive and (b) out of jail.

I added a role-playing section, where students would be armed with a rubber dummy gun, and then we'd run through various scenarios. I'd usually play the bad guy and enlist other students to act out various roles. Sometimes the answer was to shoot, but usually the answer was to avoid or deescalate. Then the entire class would discuss the decision-making process and why they did what they did. I used this to challenge the students' preconceived notions of how "their gunfight" was going to unfold. I lost track of how many times I had somebody who'd already been through a state-mandated CCW class come up to me afterward and comment about how eye-opening the scenario training was.

You might be thinking, *Wow that sounds great. Let's make all the basic training that good.* Except I did that because I wanted to, and the students were there voluntarily for that extra time. If the state made that sort of thing legally required, the mass-produced version would start to suck like all mandatory training does, and it would just become a longer exercise in box checking.

That's classroom. For states that require actual shooting portions, lazy instructors love qualifiers, because they can simply check off a list and feel like they're accomplishing something. Two shots at five yards. Check. Good shooting instructors actually take the time to watch students, they have the experience and awareness to diagnose students' weaknesses, and then they help them individually get better.

If anything, passing a basic qualifier is harmful in that it provides a false sense of security. I saw this all the time when working with law enforcement. "I passed my shooting qual in POST! I already know how to shoot good!" they'd exclaim, not realizing that the qualifier they passed was relatively easy and usually designed for the lowest common denominator to pass.

So make the tests harder, right? Except super in-depth qualifiers for regular citizens assuage the conscience of bureaucrats, and that's about it. You will often see articles lamenting the terrible hit ratios for police in gun fights, and then they extrapolate out from there that if even trained police miss a lot, how much worse will civilians be? Well, first, people miss because gunfights are *hard*. Second, most of the cops with those infamously lousy hit rates come from programs where their training consists of the same type of BS qualifiers that the bureaucrats want to force on CCW holders.

Cops are supposed to respond, chase down criminals, and arrest them. That's the opposite of what armed citizens do. The vast majority of the time, just producing the gun solves the problem for the regular gun owner. Or the violent encounter happens so close that fine marksmanship doesn't matter. So why exactly should we put some extra hoops for the permit holder to jump through, that don't really matter, don't really help, and just add one more expense to getting the permit to begin with?

The more training you mandate, the more it costs in time and money to check those boxes. So now the rich guy who can easily afford time off work to go to his nearby shooting range that has instructors on staff can exercise his rights. But the poor single mom who lives in the city that drove off all its shooting ranges can't afford the days off. No rights for her. Oh well. Too bad she has a stalker. If he shows up again, she should just call 911 and hope.

If you've already got the law written so that it requires a shooting portion, what is to keep some future anti-gun bureaucrat who hates the idea of regular people being armed from tweaking the test to make it so difficult nobody can pass it? And even if it is only as difficult as the qual for, say, the old air marshal test (which is the only federal qual I've ever shot that's legitimately challenging), and you personally are a badass gunslinger killer of cardboard, do you want to force that requirement on your mom? Sorry, Mom, you don't get to carry a gun to use at conversational distance against a rapist, because I don't feel safe knowing you can't shoot the SEAL Team Six pistol qual.

Also note that the people who are in favor of more training and tougher tests don't want to set the bar so high that they can't personally reach it. They would much rather set the bar just below what they can do, because obviously, that's how proficient you should be. Anybody who can't shoot as good as they can is obviously a menace to society. It's like the old joke, anybody who drives slower than you is a loser, and anybody who drives faster is a maniac.

When people who are nominally on my side tell me that they want mandatory training to weed out the unworthy, I'll tell them *Sure, let's do that. Except I think you should shoot at least as good as me* (and odds are that since I'm a fanatic who used to do this for a living, and has my own private shooting range at my house, I'm way better than they are). *I'll make a super test that only hardcore shooters with big practice-ammo budgets can pass. So no permit for you. That'll keep out the riffraff.*

Such as them.

Yeah, they don't like that idea.

That's basically what this fixation on mandatory training comes down to. *Feelings.* There are some on the pro-gun side who are no different from the anti-gunners who want to ban everything because it makes them feel unsafe. Regardless of your feelings, show me the numbers. If mandatory training made a huge difference in safety, how come in Alaska and Vermont, with no required training, their permit holders were about as safe as in Utah with our class that you could get through in a minimum of four hours, or states like Arizona that used to require a mandatory (if I recall correctly) sixteen hours of training?[17]

I already told you the answer. People who care, care. People who don't, don't.

Over the last decade, states slowly caught onto this, and more of them have passed constitutional carry, requiring no training or license at all. Fully half of the states have some version of this now and it is wonderful, because your rights shouldn't depend on someone else's feelings.

"Doesn't Matter. I Don't Like Them. We Should Ban Them and Take Them All Away Like Other Civilized Countries! They Don't Have Crime/Murder/Mass Killings Like We Do!"

Well, I suppose if your need to Do Something overrides all reason and logic, then by all means let's ban guns. Other nations have banned guns, why can't we?

I hate comparing the United States to other countries, because they simply aren't us. These comparisons are always terribly flawed, as cherry-picked crime stats from the socially, culturally, and economically diverse U.S. are compared to their idealized version of some super-homogenous, tiny-population Nordic nation that's exciting as oatmeal.

But since this is inevitably going to get brought up by the ignorant or dishonest, here we go.

If you go by media talking points, America is the murder capital of the universe. This is so pervasive that Europeans on Twitter will talk about how they're terrified to come to America because surely they'll get shot to death as soon as they get off the plane.

If you look at the per capita murder rates by country, depending on which source you use, America is usually toward the middle, with legendarily violent third world nations at the top, and tiny resort countries at the bottom. Not that anybody should trust what other countries claim as their crime stats, because everybody compiles their stats by different criteria, and some just outright lie for propaganda purposes. Personally I have a hard time believing that Sierra Leon is four times safer than the United States, and according to China they have almost no murders, but we all know what Mark Twain said about statistics.[18]

America's overall murder rate is also extremely misleading, but we'll get to that.

Giant, chaotic, melting-pot America has a complicated history of social volatility that has more in common with Mexico or Brazil than Norway, but the anti-gun zealots never want to compare those stats. Go figure.

They love to use Australia though. Australia had a mass killing and instituted a massive gun ban and confiscation—a program that simply would not work here, but let's run with it anyway. As anti-gun zealots like to point out, Australia hasn't had any similar events since. However, they didn't really have any before that either. You need to keep in mind that mass killings are horrific headline-grabbing statistical anomalies. And Australia has a population of twenty-six million. The United States has nearly thirteen times more people.[19]

So the big thing they didn't have before hasn't happened again. But if the Australian population is disarmed and criminals still exist, what happens without those defensive gun uses by regular citizens we talked about earlier?

Australia smokes the United States when it comes to assault and rape rates. They are assault and rape champions. Again, stats comparing different countries are notoriously unreliable because of different reporting parameters or outright propaganda, but though you might be less likely to get shot in that gun-free paradise, you're a lot more likely to get raped or beaten. Australia is *way* above the world average.[20]

Personally, I'm in favor of rapists getting shot by their intended victims. Apparently the Australian government disagrees with me on that. We also diverge on prison camps for sick people, but I'm trying not to get into politics other than guns. Of course most of the articles about Australia's crime rate will declare that this has nothing to do with regular citizens no longer being able to defend themselves.

So then we've got England, where they reacted swiftly after a mass shooting, banned and confiscated firearms, and since then their violent crime rates have risen dramatically.[21] During the same timeframe, America became increasingly well armed and our violent crime rates were trending downward—until "fiery but mostly peaceful" 2020 at least—and Britain's were rising. Their violent crime rate is somewhere between four and six times worse than ours, and Britain is notorious for underreporting their violent crime statistics.[22]

Like Australia, a cursory Google search about Britain's crime will find their ludicrous stats, yet also plenty of articles from their blatant anti-gun media outlets declaring that the increase totally has nothing to do with their regular citizens no longer being allowed to defend themselves...Sensing a trend yet?

So gun control hinders regular citizens and emboldens run-of-the-mill criminals, but surely it stops mass killers?

Not particularly. Take Norway with its extremely strict gun control for example. Their gun control laws are simply incomprehensible to most Americans. Not only that, they have been a well-off, tiny-population, ethnically and socially homogeneous country, without our gang violence or drug problems. Their gun control laws are draconian by our standards. They make Chicago look like Boise.

Surely that level of gun control will stop mass killers! Except of course for 2011 when a maniac killed 77 and injured 242 people, a body count that is absurdly high.[23]

Ironically, as I went to confirm the information about the event in 2011 and plugged "Norway mass shooting" into my search engine, I saw that there had just been another one in June 2022, when an Iranian immigrant in Oslo attacked a gay club.[24] Which again demonstrates that the silly narrative that this kind of thing only happens in America is a pathetic lie.

In 2015 a group of terrorists attacked Paris, killing 130 people and wounding at least another 350 (with some estimates nearing 500). These mass killers used illegal guns and homemade explosives.[25] Make guns harder to get, and explosives become the weapon of choice. Please do keep in mind that the largest and most advanced military coalition in human history was basically stymied for a decade by a small group using high school level chemistry and the Afghani equivalent of Radio Shack.

And if they don't want to bother getting guns or explosives, they can use a common truck as their murder weapon, like the bastard who killed 86 and injured 458 men, women, and children in Nice by driving down sidewalks.[26]

Because once again, repeat it with me, criminals simply do not give a crap. And it is even worse when the criminals are in your government, which is why it always amuses me that gun controllers want to compare the United States to the world's softest nations, and not the hyper-violent ones where the disarmed populace is endlessly abused with impunity by organized crime or its own corrupt government.

Some of the biggest mass killers in modern history have used bombs, arson, or even airliners. There is no law you can pass, no one thing you can ban, and nothing you can say or do that will stop some men from choosing evil. In 1990, 87 people were killed when an arsonist set fire to the Happy Land Nightclub in New York.[27] Forty-four were killed by a homemade bomb at a school in Bath, Michigan, and that was in 1927 when anybody could buy machine guns through the mail.[28]

It disgusts me when I see ignorant posturing about how mass killings are a uniquely American problem. No. Sorry. We don't hold the patent on depraved madness or cruelty. I understand why people are duped into believing this though. Our media fixates on any of our crimes that it thinks can be used for political gain, barely mentions any crimes that happen in the western world, and then the rest of the planet might as well not even exist at all for how little time our media spends on them. They might get an article or two, and maybe a mention on the cable news, and then it's gone.

Just a month ago as I write this, at least 50 were killed in a massacre at a Catholic church in Nigeria.[29] In 2020, 29 were killed and 58 wounded by a lone killer at a Buddhist temple in Thailand.[30] In gun-free Japan in 2019, some maniac killed 33 by setting an anime studio on fire.[31] In 2016, also in Japan, 19 residents of a care center were *stabbed to death* by a disgruntled former employee.[32]

There are hundreds of these from all over the world. Don't take my word for it. Go look for yourself, pick a continent, enter the continent and "mass killing" into your search engine, and get ready to be disturbed by the fallen nature of mankind.

And just like we see in America, the key determinate of how many people get hurt during these events is how long it takes before the killer receives a violent response.

In 2019 gunmen stormed a Kenyan hotel, killing 21, only to be stopped by the ultimate example of a "good guy with a gun," when a member of the British SAS who was shopping nearby ran back to his car, grabbed his icky, scary assault rifle, and then took care of business. Our media was forced to cover this one because the pictures of this badass in his plate carrier, balaclava, and jeans went viral.[33] On the other hand, in 2013, 67 were killed at a mall in Kenya. That one really didn't get a lot of American news coverage, but it was civilian competition shooters from the local IDPA club who showed up to fight the bad guys, and our media really despises that concept.[34]

So gun control disarms regular people, which makes them easier for regular criminals to victimize, and it does pretty much zilch against dedicated mass killers.

But now let's go back to that part about how America is so incredibly violent compared to the rest of the world. We've already seen that we're more toward the middle of the bell curve, but people forget just how vast and diverse America is. Depending on which set of stats you use, America's murder rate is somewhere around 5 per 100,000.[35]

Detroit's is 41. Birmingham's is 50. Baltimore's is 58. And Saint Louis is at 64.[36]

Yeah, that'll mess up an average. The county I live in now is point zero something, because we've only had a couple murders since cowboy times.

But it is actually even worse than you are thinking. It's not just some American cities that are cesspools of violent crime where you are far more likely to get shot. It's specific neighborhoods within those cities. For example Chicago doesn't even make the top ten list for bad crime rates, with its 18 per 100,000. Except Chicago has a giant population of around 2.6 million, and when you pull up the homicide map of the city it becomes abundantly clear that most of it is fairly quiet (by Chicago standards at least), with a handful of neighborhoods that are basically war zones.[37]

I knew a guy who grew up in one of those neighborhoods. He joined the army and said Afghanistan was more peaceful.

Back in the '90s I lived in north Birmingham, Alabama, and the local paper ran an article called "If Murder Had a Zip Code," and that zip code was where I lived. The map of the city was just like the Chicago example, with clusters of murders all concentrated in a few small, specific geographic areas, and the locals could even narrow the problem areas down to the specific blocks. You stay away from those, you're probably fine. You go near the Brick Yard (a legendarily violent public housing complex), you're gonna get shot.

Because of this insanely lopsided distribution, it's the case that most of the U.S. states will be relatively peaceful, but their cities will be worse, and a few parts of those cities are murder central. Despite the crazy mass killings getting all the coverage, most of America's shootings are good old-fashioned gang- and drug-related violence.

The reasons our violent crime is so incredibly concentrated to a handful of zip codes are beyond the scope of this book and not my area of expertise. People can argue about generational poverty, or lack of opportunity, or institutional inequality, or whatever, but the one thing I can tell you with absolute certainty is that Chicago's murders have absolutely nothing to do with my owning guns in rural Utah.

The low-crime-rate part of America is armed to the teeth. Most of our violent crime comes from our big blue cities, most of which have been totally dominated by a single political party going back generations. These cities are also the traditional home of America's strictest gun control laws and harshest enforcement thereof.

So you'll have to forgive the rest of us if we don't feel like being disarmed—allowing us to be victimized easier—in your hopeless crusade to fix the awful problems the people you voted for created where you live.

And all of that is irrelevant, because actually trying to ban and confiscate all the scary guns in America will be national suicide.

"We Should Register All the Guns!"

This Do-Something isn't as common as it once was, just because most anti-gunners are so uninformed that they already think this is a thing. In reality very few jurisdictions in America have any sort of gun registration, but Hollywood is so out of touch that they'll have a show about a murder in Wyoming and have dialog about checking to see who the gun is registered to.

There is no federal registry for regular firearms. The only federal registration is for things that fall under the NFA (legal machine guns, "short-barrel rifles and shotguns," suppressors, et cetera), and the state of the registry for even that relatively tiny number of items is a mess, with the government requiring months and sometimes years to process transfers.

Only seven states and the District of Columbia have some form of gun registration. Of course, it's the usual suspects that have all the other ridiculous laws, but still have plenty of crime.[38]

Since most firearms used in criminal activity are illegally obtained, it doesn't really matter who the original purchaser was before it got burgled. Unless you are one of those really horrible people who want to hold law-abiding citizens responsible for crimes committed with property stolen from them—but that's so insanely vile that only the most fanatical anti-gunners ever suggest it.

Registries have also been used for malicious abuse, with the private data of gun owners and permit holders getting leaked. At the time of my writing this, there are breaking reports that this has happened again in California, where the state released the private personal information of every single permit holder, as well as everyone who applied for a permit over the last ten years.[39]

That's supposed to be private information. Now some of the people on that list will get harassed for their beliefs or possibly targeted in other ways. Getting outed as not just a gun owner, but someone who wants to carry a gun, is career death in some industries. This is also a great list for burglars who now know which addresses have valuable guns to steal. The timing of this "leak" is extra suspicious, considering that it happened immediately after a landmark Supreme Court decision that smacked down bigoted, corrupt, pay-to-play concealed carry licensing schemes like California's.

Registration is stupid, but it is also one of those lines that most American gun owners will refuse to cross for one very good reason. There is a common saying that *registration leads to confiscation.* The government can never seize them all if they don't know who has what. The countries I talked about in the last section with bans and confiscations had registries first, that way the authorities knew who to go after. Tyrants love having a handy list of which of their political opponents are armed and a potential nuisance. If a government ever wants to abuse some section of your populace, a registry is a wonderful to-do list of who to target first.

Which brings us into the biggest, scariest, Do-Something there is. Confiscation.

"You Crazy Gun Nuts and Your Dumb Second Amendment, We Should Just Confiscate All the Guns Once and for All!"

Many of you may truly believe that. You may think that the Second Amendment is archaic, outdated, and totally pointless. However about half the country vehemently disagrees with you, and of them, a pretty large portion is fully willing to shoot somebody in defense of it. We've already covered how your partial bans are stupid and don't do anything, so unless you are merely a hypocrite more interested in style rather than results, the only way to achieve your ultimate goal is to come and take our guns away.

So let's talk about confiscation. This is the part where we delve into what the Second Amendment is *really* about.

In 2018 a U.S. congressman embarrassed himself on Twitter. Eric Swalwell (D-CA)—who is best known for his relationship with a Communist Chinese spy and farting on live TV[40]—got into a debate about gun control, suggested a mandatory buyback (which is basically confiscation with a happy face sticker on it), and when someone told him that they would resist, he said resistance was futile because the government has nukes.[41]

And everybody sane was like, *Wait, what?*

Of course the congressman backpedaled. You see, using nuclear weapons on American gun owners was an exaggeration, he just wanted to rhetorically demonstrate that the all-powerful federal government could crush us peasants like bugs (they hold our pathetic lives in their iron hand), and he'd never ever advocate for the use of nuclear weapons on American soil (that would be bad for the environment!), and instead he merely wants to send a SWAT team to your house to shoot you in the face if you don't comply.

See? That's way better.

But this isn't about that particular tweet from one idiot congressman. This goofy line of reasoning pops up constantly.

For example, there was a meme with a picture of an Apache attack helicopter with the super pithy caption, "I see you keep an AR-15 in case you need to show the government who's the boss...Hi, I'm Uncle Sam and I keep of whole fleet of AH-64 helicopter gunships in case I need to show Freedom Eagle Dot Facebook who's the boss."

I've seen these for nukes, drones, tanks, or cruise missiles. Sadly, this is one of the better ones, but that's because the Left can't meme. It's a popular media soundbite too, all based on the same flawed premise. The federal government has access to advanced weapon systems, and thus anyone who resisted gun confiscation would be effortlessly destroyed by them, ergo gun control has already won—forgone conclusion—and they declare victory.

Like most political memes, they're taking an extremely complex situation and providing a cartoonish, simplistic answer, which makes them look like clowns to anybody with a clue, but scores them lots of virtue-signal points with their likewise ignorant but posturing friends. To my people, this is really goofy stuff. If you have even a basic knowledge of this topic, these memes are about as clever as the ones from the flat Earth society.

Americans are so divided on guns it's like we're speaking two different languages, but when it comes to outright confiscation, we are on two different planets. To parse this one in the style of the rest of our Do-Somethings:

"The Idea of the Second Amendment Being Used to Stand against a Tyrannical Government Is Obsolete, Because Our Federal Government Is Too Overwhelmingly Powerful for Its Citizens to Resist."

To those of you who really believe that, I'm going to try to not be too insulting. Accent on *try*. But I'll probably fail because this is a really stupid argument.

My last regular job before becoming a full-time author was in the proverbial "Evil Military Industrial Complex" as a contractor, where I helped maintain those various advanced weapon systems you expect to bomb me with. Before that I sold the guns you want to confiscate to the people you want to bomb, and I also sold them to the people you want to do the bombing for you.

On that note, I don't think you fully comprehend the nature of the individuals you expect to do your dirty work, but I'll come back around to that in a bit.

First let's talk about the basic premise that an irregular force primarily armed with rifles would be helpless against a powerful army that has things like drones and attack helicopters. This is a deeply ironic argument to make, considering that the most techno-logically advanced military coalition in history spent the better part of the last two decades fighting goat herders with AKs in Afghani-stan and Iraq. Seriously, it's like you guys only pay attention to American casualties when there's a Republican in office and an election coming up.

Nobel Peace Prize–winner Barack Obama launched over five hundred drone strikes during his eight years in office.[42] We've used jets, smart bombs, tanks, I don't know how many thousands of raids on homes and compounds, all the stuff that the anti-gun memes say they're willing to do to crush the gun nuts, and we've spent something like $8 trillion on the global war on terror so far.[43]

Despite all that we pulled out of Afghanistan in a giant embarrassing trainwreck of an evacuation, and the Taliban is still there, now offi-cially running the country. Or did you guys already memory hole all that?

Russia was supposed to steamroll the Ukraine in seventy-two hours. How's that working out? It's not like Vietnam was that long ago either.

So yes, groups of irregular locals can be a real pain in the ass to a technologically superior military force. That's pretty obvious.

Now here is the interesting part. Estimates are that at any given time in Iraq we were fighting about 20,000 insurgents.[44] Keep that number in mind, because now we're going to talk about the scope of this hypothetical fight over gun control in America.

Nobody really knows how many people in America own guns, or how many guns are here. The estimates range wildly. I've noticed a trend over recent years of the vulture media trying to minimize that number, to make it seem like it's actually a very low percentage of Americans who own firearms, a fading cultural anomaly if you will, and to try and explain away the two to four *million* new background checks done every month for new purchases—to make it seem like it's just a handful of us who own a few hundred guns each.

Uh-huh.... Sure.

While trying to make gun ownership seem like an oddball thing, I've seen the media come up with some truly silly estimates about the total number of guns in this country. A common estimate that is really easy to debunk is the 400 million number that gets tossed out a lot. That's derived from the number of NICS (National Instant Criminal Background Check System) requests.[45]

The problem is that doesn't take into account the tens of millions of guns sold before that (and they never really wear out), the fact that one NICS check can be used to buy multiples at a time (two or three is common, but you can do more, and the most I know of on one check was twelve), and that many U.S. states (including the gun nuttiest) use their own state background check systems—and I'm unsure which of those are added to that federal number.

That number also doesn't account for all the homemade guns. If you build it at home and keep it for yourself, it never needs a background check. Advances in cheap home machining had been making that far more common, and then 3D printing came along and it really blew up.

When pollsters call to ask us if we own guns and how many guns we own, we think about things like a congressman talking about nuking us—and immediately lie our asses off. The biggest recurring joke in the gun community is that "I don't own any guns, because I lost them all in a freak canoe accident."

To really understand those NICS numbers (and to put to bed that whole silly idea that gun ownership is limited to a handful of us who own piles of them), look at recent years, pick out the biggest sales months of all time, and then think about what current events were happening during those months. The government was locking everything down.

The populace was afraid. Then we had the "fiery but mostly peaceful" protests, while the nervous populace watched and learned that they could get their houses burned down or get beaten to death in the streets while the cops watched, afraid to get involved.

Some gun stores had lines out the door and down the sidewalks of people desperately trying to get their hands on whatever they could in order to protect themselves. Inventory was low. Dealers were selling whatever they could get in as fast as they could get it. Millions of guns were being bought every week. With high demand and limited supply, prices skyrocketed . . .

And guys like me don't pay scalper's prices for guns. We've already got ours. Most of those sales were to first timers. My local dealer's walls were bare for months at a time, as he sold guns so fast there was no time to unpack them and put them on display. A giant portion of those sales were to newbs. It turns out not wanting to be murdered while the law takes a holiday is a great motivator to arm up.

So nobody really knows how many guns there are in the United States, or how many of us own them. But the answer is A LOT.

The *Washington Post* ran an article called "Americans Vastly Overestimate the Number of Gun Owners." As with most *WaPo* articles, it was mostly nonsense, but they came to the asinine conclusion that *only* 20–30 percent of Americans own guns.[46] That may sound plausible if you never venture out of Manhattan, but out here in flyover country, that's downright laughable. To make this hypothetical mass gun confiscation as achievable as possible, let's run with their ludicrous estimate. We'll even take the lower one of 20 percent.

Too bad America has over a third of a billion people, because even the unrealistic figure of twenty percent of 338 million is still a whopping 67 million people. That's about the same as the entire population of France. That's about the same as the population of the United

Kingdom, only with five hundred times the firepower. Good thing we didn't go with that 30 percent, because now the number is way bigger than the population of Germany, and you know what a pain beating them was last time.

It's kind of funny, when it comes to us adopting social or economic programs, American progressives are always comparing the United States to Sweden, which has the population of LA County, and that's totally not apples and oranges, but declaring war on a percentage of the American population bigger than most NATO states? That's no biggie.

But I digress...

Okay, so let's say Congressman Swalwell gets his wish and the government says, *Turn them in or else*. And even though the government has become tyrannical enough to send SWAT teams door-to-door and threaten citizens with drones and attack helicopters, rather than half the states saying, *Up yours, this means Civil War 2*, instead we'll stick to the rosiest of all possible outcomes and stipulate that most gun owners comply.

In fact, let's be super kind. Rather than a realistic number, like half or a third of those people getting really, really pissed off and hoisting the black flag, let's say that 90 percent of them decide to totally put all their faith into the government and hope that the all-powerful entity that just threatened to kill their entire family will never ever turn tyrannical from now on, pinky swear. So what do they have to lose? And a whopping 90 percent of gun owners go along peacefully.

That means you are only dealing with over six and a half MILLION insurgents. The entire active U.S. military is about 1.3 million, with about an 800,000 reserve.[47] This is also assuming that those two Venn diagrams don't overlap, which is just plain idiotic, but I'll get to that too.

Sure, you'd have to pull out the really young and really old, but this is all hypothetical math anyway. So let's be super generous—I'm talking absurdly generous—and say that a full 99 percent of these 67 million problematic gun owners say, *Won't somebody think of the children?* and they all hold hands and sing kumbaya, so that then you are only dealing with the angriest disgruntled malcontents who hate progress...These are those crazy, knuckle-dragging bastards that you will have to put in the ground.

And there are 677,000 of them.

To put that into perspective, in any given year we were fighting about 20,000 insurgents in Iraq, a country that is roughly the size of California. This would be over thirty times as many fighters, spread across twenty-two times the area.

And that estimated number is pathetically, laughably low.

In one of the bluest states in America, the New York SAFE Act only had around a 4 percent compliance rate.[48] And that's mostly people choosing to ignore an onerous law. Because the further you get away from the major cities, the more people simply don't give a crap about your utopian foolishness. Its benign neglect, and most Americans are happy to ignore you until you mess with them. You start dropping Hellfire missiles on Indiana? It's game on. And that 1 percent is going to turn into 50 percent damn quick.

So by the numbers, it's an insurmountable problem, but we're just getting started with how stupid this idea is.

Let's talk about the logistical challenges of this holy crusade to free the country of icky guns and murder everybody who thinks differently than you do.

In Iraq our troops operated from a few secure bases. Those were the big areas where we could do things like store supplies, airlift things in or out, repair vehicles, and have field hospitals, a Burger King, et cetera. And then there were forward operating bases. These are the little camps troops could stage out of to operate in a given area. The hard part was keeping those places supplied, and I believe most of America's casualties came from convoys getting hit while trying to provide those places with things like ammo, food, and fuel, because when you're moving around, you're a vulnerable target. All of these places were secured, and if you got too close, or they thought you were going to try and drive a car bomb through the gate, they'd light you up.

Now, imagine trying to conduct operations in a place with thirty times the bad guys, and there are no "safe zones." Most of our military bases aren't out in the desert by themselves. They've had a town grow up around them, and the only thing separating the jets from the people you expect them to be bombing is a chain-link fence.

The confiscators don't live on base. They live in apartment complexes and houses in the suburbs next door to the people you expect them to murder. Every time they go out to kick in some redneck's door, their convoy is moving through an area with lots of angry people who shoot small animals from far away for fun, and the only thing they remember about chemistry class is the formula for Tannerite (that's a simple and super-easy-to-make binary explosive commonly used as a reactive target, for you non–gun culture types).

Something that I find profoundly troubling came up when I've had this discussion before: I've had a caring liberal tell me that the example of Iraq doesn't apply, because "we kept the gloves on," whereas fighting America's gun nuts would be a righteous total war with nothing held back. Wow. I've got to wonder about the mentality of people who demand rigorous ROEs to prevent civilian casualties in a foreign country but are bloodthirsty enough to carpet-bomb Texas.

You really hate us and then act confused about why we want to keep our guns? But I don't think unrelenting total war against everyone who has ever disagreed with you on Facebook is going to be quite as clean as you expect.

There will be no secure delivery of ammo, food, and fuel because the guys who build that, grow that, and ship that—well, you just dropped a Hellfire on his cousin Bill because he wouldn't turn over his SKS. Nope. Starve. And that's assuming they don't still make the delivery, but the gas is tainted and food is poisoned.

Oh wait...Poison? That would be unsportsmanlike! Really? Because your guy just brought up nuclear weapons. What? You think that you're going to declare war on half of America, with rules of engagement that would make Genghis Khan blush, and my side would keep using Marquess of Queensberry rules?

Oh hell, no.

For most people on the Left, political violence is a knob, and they can turn the heat up and down, with things like protests and riots, all the way up to destruction of property, and sometimes murder...But for the vast majority of folks on the right, it's an off-and-on switch. And the settings are "Vote" or "Shoot Everybody." And believe me, you really don't want that switch to get flipped, because Civil War 2.0 would make Bosnia look like a trip to Disneyworld.

Speaking of ugly, do you really honestly think that you're going to be able to kill people because they disagree with you, and they won't hit you back where it hurts? While you're drone striking Omaha, Nebraska, you really think that the people who live where all the food is grown, the electricity is generated, and all the freeways and rail lines run through—do you really think that some of them aren't going to take it personally? And that they're not going to use their location and access to make life extremely uncomfortable for you?

The scariest single conversation I've ever heard in my life was with five special forces guys having a fun thought exercise about how they would bring a major American city to its knees. They picked Chicago, because it was a place they'd all been. It was fascinating, and utterly terrifying. And I'll never ever put any of it in a book, because I don't want to give crazy people any ideas. Give it about a week and people would be eating each other. And gee whiz, take one wild guess what the political leanings of most Green Berets are?

I've had similar conversations with cops about how incredibly easy it would be to entirely shut down and utterly ruin their city with only a small crew of dedicated individuals and about forty-eight hours of mayhem. And guess what their political leanings were? Hint, most of them were eager to retire because they'd been treated like trash by their liberal mayors and take their pension to some place like Arkansas.

So yeah, let's talk about those people you think are going to be unfeeling automatons who will have no problem killing their friends and neighbors on your behalf...

They are us.

Above I mentioned a Venn diagram of obstinate gun owners and the military, but you can change that to cops and it's going to be pretty similar. Those groups overlap a lot, and, depending on the particular department or unit, the Venn diagrams look like stacks of pancakes.

Back when I owned a gun store, we were located one block from Utah Army National Guard Headquarters. Every drill weekend my building was a sea of ACU (and the fact that very few of my liberal readers know what that abbreviation means just goes to show how incredibly out of touch they are, but I mean the ugly sage-gray digital camouflage). It was just a bunch of guys hanging out, talking, and buying guns.

Lots and lots of guns.

I know most of the people sharing these spicy memes about attack helicopters can't tell different types of guns apart, but they were specifically buying the scary ones that the vultures want to ban the most. Thousands of them. And cops...Holy moly I sold a lot of guns to cops. Not department guns, though we supplied a few of those, but personal guns.

Having worked with a lot of police departments, guess what? The officers who actually know how to shoot? The ones who run the training programs? Usually they're my people too. The gun nuts gravitate toward that position because (a) more taxpayer-funded ammo and (b) they actually care about the subject, so they learn on their own and then try to pass those skills on to their coworkers to better keep them alive.

Whenever I see one of these goofy memes produced by some gender studies major, it just demonstrates how incredibly sheltered and out of touch these people are. They don't know anything about the military or law enforcement. Usually if they're talking about soldiers, it's about how they're evil baby killers, or time bombs of PTSD rage, or poor deluded fools who joined the military because they couldn't get a real job... And cops, it's about how they're just a bunch of trigger-happy racists itching for an excuse to execute everybody who looks different than they do.

But don't worry. Despite all those years of abuse, ACAB, and throwing Molotovs at them, when you ask them to go door-to-door in their hometown to systematically attack people they've known their whole lives (friends and family members who've done nothing wrong), and maybe get shot or blown up, and, when it's over, to then turn in their own personal guns—all because some moron in a big city a thousand miles away said so—I'm sure they'll hop right to it.

It is common to ascribe increasingly terrible things to the people you hate—like all gun owners are murderous, racist, kill-crazy, hillbilly, dumbass peckerwoods who want children to die. And you end up believing that we in the gun culture community are this unimaginable, evil "other," so it's okay to threaten to murder us with drone strikes and feel morally good about yourself. Because we're bad, and you're the good guy, and thus totally justified in dropping bombs on us.

Yet you assume that the people who gravitate toward the career fields you'll need in order to wage war on us will feel the same way you do. When in reality most of them think you're posturing, elitist, ignoramuses who don't know the first thing about guns, crime, violence, or America.

Now this is where I'll part ways with many of my libertarian brethren, because they are quick to point out that there are plenty of places where cops enforce existing gun or drug laws. The part they're missing is that most people are complicated, and they've got lines they won't cross. In this case, the target isn't some "other," it's not just their people, it's literally *them*. In an active shooting war between the government and half the population, that's a pretty big line. And we're not talking about people they are already inclined not to like, but rather they're supposed to go shoot their pediatrician and their mechanic for doing something that up until a few days ago was legal and they were doing themselves.

Obviously some percentage of the military and police will be happy to put on the jack boots and start loading people into cattle cars. But another large percentage will say, *Nope, I'm calling in sick, don't feel like getting blown up today.* And another big chunk will actively help the insurgents, *because they hate you and everything you stand for.* Like seriously, out-of-touch coastal liberals, how many small-town sheriff's deputies do you think would describe themselves as "progressive"?

Now this will vary wildly depending on jurisdiction. Some places, no problem. People will comply. Others, because of the culture, they won't. Yet, in the places where they are the most likely to resist, those are the places where you are the most likely to have the local authorities be actively on the side of the insurgents. This is kind of a no-brainer to anybody who has ever looked at any guerilla war ever in history. Which means that the occupiers then have to import outsiders to do the dirty deeds, but then the presence of outsiders pisses off the rest of the local fence-sitters, and soon everybody is getting blown up.

The problem with all those advanced weapons systems you Swalwells of the world don't understand but keep sticking into memes? Guess who builds them, maintains them, and drives them? When I first saw that idiotic Apache meme, my comment was that, sadly, Freedom Eagle's day job was as a contractor doing helicopter engine maintenance for the very military Swalwell expects to nuke Freedom Eagle.

Those drones you guys like to go on about and barely understand? One of the contracts I worked on was maintaining the servers for them. Guess which way most military contractors vote? Duh. Though honestly, if I was still in my "Evil Military Industrial Complex" job when this went down, I'd just quietly embezzle and funnel millions of DOD dollars to the rebels.

So you've got an insurmountable challenge that's logistically impossible, and a big chunk of the people you expect to fight on your behalf will either go AWOL or be actively against you. Your side would need an incredible amount of will, especially after they've turned off your electricity and water and there's no more food on the shelves.

This is why smart anti-gunners prefer to boil the frog slowly. Simple, incremental changes: the National Firearms Act, the Gun Control Act, the Assault Weapons Ban, and, more recently, red flag laws. If you push too far too fast, the frog jumps out of the pot. Except, pro-gun people have been actively pushing back and making huge gains at the state level and in the courts. Such victories by us uppity peasants frustrate imbeciles like Eric Swalwell enough to get them to say the quiet part out loud.

To pull off confiscation now you'd have to be willing to destroy the country. The congressman's take was incredibly stupid, but it was nice to see someone like that being honest about it for once. In order to maybe, hypothetically save thousands, you'd be willing to slaughter millions. Either you really suck at math, or the ugly truth is that you just hate the other side so much that you think slaughtering millions is worth it to make them fall in line. And if that's the case, you're a great example of why the rest of us aren't ever going to give up our guns.

So the real question the anti-gun, ban-and-confiscate crowd should be asking themselves is this: How many of your fellow Americans are you willing to have killed in order to bring about your utopian vision of the future?

There are a lot of people who are zealous, dumb, or crazy enough to still be in favor of outright confiscation. We see them all the time declaring their intent to pry them from our cold dead hands and so on...But we're really doubtful any of them will be volunteering to be on these confiscation squads themselves. Hence many people on my side get tired of debating with the willfully ignorant and end up telling them to "stack up."

Outside of urban enclaves, gun control is super unpopular. There is a growing movement of states and counties declaring themselves Second Amendment sanctuary zones, where they are simply going to ignore any new federal gun laws. After years of other jurisdictions flaunting federal drug and immigration laws, this development shouldn't come as a surprise.

I've seen some people on my side get all black-pilled doomer over Americans actually resisting gun confiscation, with their justification being COVID lockdowns, and how much crap regular people put up with during those. I disagree. The difference is that COVID was an unexpected surprise, where people were terrified, and there was a lot of really bad information floating around so even the skeptical were still worried enough to go along. Then after a few months of millions of us not dying from an unstoppable plague, most of the country got tired of it and moved on with life. Rural America and many states went back to normal as fast as they could, while the draconian lockdowns mostly remained in the same kinds of urban jurisdictions that love them some gun control.

Gun control is something that we've been debating forever, and for the potential resisters I'm talking about, confiscation is a line they drew in the sand a long time ago. Americans will put up with a lot of nonsense—especially when they're unsure about it—but crossing that line is a symbol that the social contract has been irreparably broken. There's no turning back. There's nothing left to lose.

To many Americans, the Second Amendment is the proverbial big red button. It's behind a sheet of glass that says Break Only in Case of Emergency. It's the last-ditch kill switch on the American experiment. Because if a nation as powerful as ours ever goes fully tyrannical, God help us all.

Nobody sane actually wants to have to push this button. Hot heads say, *If not now, when?* But they say that every time something happens that they don't like. It is a valid question to ask though.

There's the old saying about the boxes of liberty, with various versions attributed to different originators going back to the 1830s. The common one is "There are four boxes to be used in the defense of liberty: soap, ballot, jury, and ammo. Please use in that order."

This book is about guns, not every divisive political topic in the country, but there is a lot of wisdom to that quote. It is my fervent hope that the American people and our elected leaders follow that order, and don't leave a critical mass feeling like the first three don't work anymore.

■ ■ ■

So that is the exhaustive list of Do-Somethings.

In conclusion, it doesn't really matter which one they run with when politicians and pundits start screaming *we've got to do something*! Because in reality, most of them already know about the issues I've listed. They know their scams don't work. They just don't care. The ones who walk around with their security details of well-armed men in their well-guarded government buildings don't give a damn about stopping evil criminals and mass murderers. They care about getting themselves more power and increasing their control over you.

They don't care if you get killed. In fact, they'll disarm you, then utterly fail to protect you, and after you get murdered and left in a gutter, they'll use your death for clout.

If a bad guy used a gun with a big magazine, ban magazines. If instead he used more guns, ban owning multiple guns. If he used a more powerful gun with less shots, ban powerful guns. If he ignored some gun-free zone, make more places gun-free zones. If he killed a bunch of innocents, make sure you disarm the innocents even harder for next time. Just in case, let's ban other guns that weren't even involved in any crimes, just because they're too big, too small, too ugly, too cute, too long, too short, too fat, too thin—and if you think I'm joking, there's either been a law or proposed law for each of those—but most of all ban anything that makes some politician irrationally afraid, which is pretty much everything.

They will never be satisfied. In countries where they have already banned guns, now they are banning knives and putting cameras on every street. They talk about compromise, but it is never a compromise. It is never, *Wow, gun people, you offer some quick, easy, inexpensive, viable defenses, let's try those.* Instead it is always, *What can we take from you this time?* Or, *What will enable us to make some office of the state even more powerful?*

Then regular criminals will go on still not caring, the next aspiring mass murderer will watch the last one briefly become the most famous person in the world, the media will keep on vilifying the people who actually do the most to defend the innocent, the ignorant will call guys like me names and tell us we must like dead babies, while nothing actually changes to better protect anyone.

Chapter Six

Good Guys with Guns

We've covered why the usual anti-gun Do-Somethings accomplish nothing or actively make the problem worse. Now I want to go over some of the things we can do to help keep people safe from violent criminals while still protecting Americans' civil liberties. Starting at the individual, personal level.

Get armed. Get trained. Get involved.

For some of you, I'm preaching to the choir. You're already armed, you've got your ducks in a row, your hardware and software are squared away, and you are politically active for gun rights. That's fantastic. You have a golden opportunity to be an ambassador and an example to others. To those who aren't there yet, or who are on the fence about armed self-defense, I want to make the case and then help you get started down the right path. For the handful of hardened anti-gunners who have made it this far, I hope you'll keep an open mind. I don't expect you to suddenly have a turn of heart and go gun shopping, but if you'd quit actively trying to punish the rest of us for the actions of others, that would be great!

Get Armed

I'm not a lawyer and this isn't legal advice. The laws for buying, owning, and carrying firearms vary by jurisdiction, and even mostly sane places sometimes have some peculiarities, so you will need to figure out what the rules are where you live. Your local FFL can be a great resource to walk you through the process for your area; however, this is how it basically works in most of the country.

If you are entirely new to this, the first time you walk into a gun store might be a little overwhelming. There's a lot of things to choose from and a lot of bad information out there. I don't know your needs, and this a book is about gun control, not a buyer's guide. My recommendation is figure out what you want to use the gun for—home defense, concealed carry, hunting some specific animal, fun at the range, the end of the world as we know it, et cetera—and that will narrow it down to types. Then pick one of the reputable name brands that is in your budget. Do your homework first, but keep in mind everybody on the internet is biased somehow.

Like I talked about in the section on background checks, to purchase a firearm from a dealer you will be required to fill out paperwork, present ID, and then the FFL will call in a background check. You can now pay for it and take it home.

Congratulations, you are now a gun owner. Welcome to a real big tent.

Now that you've got a gun, make sure that you are storing it so that it is safe and accessible only to you and whomever else you authorize to use it. How you do that will depend entirely on the nature of your home and who lives there. This is especially important if you have young children.

One note on securing firearms around children. Remember when you were a kid and your dad told you to stay away from *the forbidden closet of mystery?* Then what was the first thing you did once your parents weren't home? You looked to see what was in the forbidden closet of mystery. Obviously. When it comes to kids and firearms, don't make the gun some secret, taboo thing. Remove the mystery. Show it to them. Explain it to them. Then they won't be all curious and inclined to try and mess with it while you're gone.

It isn't enough to just have a firearm, you need to be responsible and learn how to use it safely. You need hardware and software.

Get Trained

I actually recommend starting the learning process long before buying a firearm, but I also know that's not how most people who get into guns later in life do it. Something happens to shake your worldview, you feel the need to defend yourself, so you go out and buy a gun...and then the realization dawns, what now? Irresponsible morons just load it and leave it unsecured in their sock drawer, assuming that when the time comes they'll magically know how to use it, but that's just a catastrophe waiting to happen.

On the most basic, fundamental level, you need to know the four basic rules of gun safety. Different organizations and instructors have different wordings for these, but the fundamentals are the same. Memorize these. Live these. Treat these like religious commandments from on high, and you'll never shoot yourself or someone else on accident.

- **Always keep your firearm pointed in the safest possible direction.** Don't let your muzzle cover anything you're not willing to kill or destroy. When you have a weapon in your hand, be hypervigilant about what you are pointing it at, especially your own body parts!
- **Assume all guns are loaded.** If you see a firearm, assume it's loaded. Never take anyone's word for a gun's status.

Even if you have checked the chamber and magazine for yourself and confirmed it is empty, still treat it like it is loaded. That builds good, safe habits for the day you pick one up that isn't supposed to be loaded but is. What do people say after they screw up and have a negligent discharge? "I thought it was empty."

- **Keep your finger off the trigger until you are ready to shoot.** Guns don't shoot themselves. Find a tactile spot on the gun outside of the trigger guard where you can consistently keep your finger indexed straight. And keep it there until you are actively engaging the target. As soon as you're done shooting, your finger goes back to that same safe index position. I want this to be so ingrained that when you pick up a cordless drill or a squirt gun your finger is indexed safely.

- **Be sure of your target and what's around and behind it.** Know your target and its environment. You are responsible for every bullet that leaves your gun. Make sure you know where that bullet is going to land.

I could talk about each of these a lot more, but this is a political book, not a learn-to-shoot book; however, following these rules is so absolutely vital that I'm including them here. If you don't care enough to learn anything else about guns, at least memorize these. Even if you despise guns, learn these.

Seek out quality instruction but be aware that not all trainers are created equal. There are a lot of YouTube channels and magazine articles giving advice, but those vary wildly in quality based on the creator. Getting advice from the internet isn't ideal, but I also recognize it is what most Americans are going to do. Keep an open mind, use your critical thinking skills, and take everything anyone tells you with a grain of salt.

In-person instruction is better. It's more hands on, and a good teacher will be able to help you with your specific needs. Your local gun stores and ranges will often have the contact info for the instructors working in your area. Then there are high quality, well-known firearms instructors and facilities throughout America, and if you don't live near one of these, many of them travel to different ranges that host them around the country. Classes like this range from super basic to extremely advanced.

Even if you have had some training, don't stop. Keep learning. I've been doing this for a long time, and I still try to take a couple of gun classes a year to keep from getting complacent. Plus, gun school is fun.

Local competition clubs are another fantastic resource for new shooters. Check at your nearby ranges to see what shooting organizations compete in your area. You don't need to jump right in, as even watching can be educational. These events are sports, not training for a gun fight, but competition shooters can *shoot*. And many of them are happy to give advice and steer newbies in the right direction.

Then there are your state concealed weapons classes. This is not about keeping a gun in your home, but actually carrying one in public. However, much of the information they cover will apply to both, especially when it comes to your state's laws concerning the use of force. Even if you're not planning on carrying a gun yet, I still recommend taking your state's class. It's worth it just for the information alone.

Traditionally there have been three types of concealed carry laws in America: constitutional carry, shall issue, and may issue.

"Constitutional carry" basically means that any law-abiding citizen has the right to carry a gun concealed without getting a permit first. However constitutional carry states usually still offer a concealed weapons permit to their residents because there are some perks to having one, like reciprocity, which means other states honor your state's permit, so you can carry in that other state as well.

"Shall issue" means that the state will provide a permit to carry a concealed firearm to anyone who meets the basic legal requirements. These states all have some form of educational requirement, usually in the form of a CCW class.

"May issue" means that those in state government will provide a permit to carry a concealed firearm *if they feel like it*. Yes. You read that right. Permits exist there, and you can apply to get one; however, some specific government employee has to okay it. What this often turns into is is a situation where regular people are out of luck, but movie stars, politicians, and rich CEOs can get one. So if you can donate $15,000 to a city councilman, you get rights, and the peasants can die in a gutter. May issue is a vile disgrace, where only the rich and politically connected can defend themselves and everyone else is a second-class citizen.

Luckily there are now two kinds of CCW laws, because with the recent *New York State Rifle & Pistol Association, Inc. v. Bruen* decision at the Supreme Court, may issue got taken behind the barn like Old Yeller. And if you're not old enough to get that reference, SCOTUS declared may issue–style concealed carry laws to be unconstitutional. This decision has huge ramifications along several avenues of the gun rights battle that we will talk about more later.

As of the time of writing this book, the blue states that practiced that horrible system are writing new laws. Considering how much New York and California hate their gun owners, those new laws will probably still be horrible, but in other exciting ways.

The nice thing about CCW classes is that they are common, relatively cheap, easy to find, and all of them in your state are working off the same basic framework. They are a good place to start, but a terrible place to stop. I *taught* hundreds of these, and I'm still continuing my education.

Seek out training opportunities whenever you can, and never stop learning.

Get Involved

When I first got into gun rights activism as a young man, it felt like we were in a losing battle. There was a nonsensical federal assault weapons ban. Many states didn't allow people to carry guns at all, and even in the good ones it was still an onerous process to get a permit. The media was waging a relentless culture war against us and winning. Too many politicians and even lobbying organizations that were supposedly on our side were quick to compromise. And by compromise I mean the anti-gun zealots would demand everything and get some of it, while we'd get nothing except the knowledge that they would come for the rest next time.

People who haven't been involved in this as long don't realize just how doomed we felt. The general vibe was, *What's the point?* The ATF could entrap you into cutting a shotgun barrel half an inch too short, and then shoot your wife because she was armed with an infant, and nobody would care. This was the same time period that a botched ATF raid in Waco, Texas, ended with the horrifyingly violent deaths of more people than have been murdered by any typical mass killer.[1] The federal leviathan was coming for our guns, and we all knew it.

Except things began to change. State organizations started making gains. Lawsuits were filed and won. The gun culture became less insular and defensive, and more open and assertive. The internet made coordination between gun rights activists and regular gun owners easier, and elected officials started hearing from an increasing number of voters who were sick of being punished because some stranger they had nothing to do with had done something bad.

When the Assault Weapons Ban sunsetted, Americans rushed out to buy the very guns they had been told they couldn't have for the previous decade, and millions discovered that these so-called "assault weapons" were great. What had once been a niche-type firearm for connoisseurs surged in popularity and is now the most common type of rifle in the country.

There was a major SCOTUS decision reaffirming that the Second Amendment meant what it said with *District of Columbia v. Heller*. This caused a pushback against harsh local laws all over the country. Concealed carry became increasingly normal. As more people did it, the hyperbolic lies about armed citizens having Wild West–style shootouts over parking spaces became a much harder sell. More states adopted CCW laws, and the states that already had them made them better. The differences between gun-friendly and gun-restricting jurisdictions became increasingly stark and obvious. The Wild West would be a huge step up in safety for many Chicago residents.

During this time the state kept on demonstrating that when the chips were down and you were in danger, you probably couldn't count on them. Each time the law stood down and let criminals act unimpeded, it created new gun owners. Nothing motivates people to learn to take care of themselves like getting left hanging in the wind.

Gun ownership has become more common, more accepted, and more understood over a much broader demographic, but we've still got a long way to go.

There are several national gun rights organizations, and most states have their own as well. I'm not going to tell you which to join. That's a decision you should make for yourself based upon which ones you think are the most worthy of your support, but I think you should join *something*.

The news media likes to talk about the NRA a lot, as if it is some massive, all-powerful, monolithic entity. The NRA makes a great boogeyman for anti-gunners, and the media always acts like gullible gun owners are led around by the NRA and we just do what it tells us to. Except they've got that totally backwards. Compared to the general sentiments of the gun culture, the NRA is *moderate.*

Personally, I donate to the Firearms Policy Coalition, because they specialize in lawsuits against jurisdictions with unconstitutional gun laws around the country. And that makes me smile.

Regardless of what organizations you choose to support, you can't expect results just from sending a check off and hoping someone else will do the work. If you want change, help out however you think you best can. Your ability to influence local politics is going to vary greatly upon where you live, but make your voice heard. If you don't have to hide your beliefs, don't. Obviously some of us live in deep blue anti-gun areas where coming out as a gun owner will get us ostracized or fired, so we'll need to be cool about it.

Make friends. Reach out and help teach others. Spread knowledge, but make sure it's good knowledge first! Network. Take new people shooting. Nothing removes the stigma quite like having fun.

The anti-gun zealots want you to feel alone and ashamed. If you believe you're in a tiny, disliked minority, despised by proper, good-thinking society, you're more likely to keep your opinion to yourself. The relentless culture war tries to portray gun owners as crazed and violent ticking time bombs of PTSD rage, or racist, knuckle-dragging, rednecks just itching to shoot somebody. They despise anything that portrays gun owners as regular, normal Americans.

Only that's exactly what we are.

So now that you're armed, learning and improving, and actively helping out, what other good things can we push for?

Do Away with Gun-Free Zones

Gun-free zones are hunting preserves for innocent people. Period.

Think about it. Imagine that you're a violent, homicidal madman, looking to make a statement and hoping to go from disaffected loser to most famous man in the world. The best way to accomplish your goals is to kill a whole bunch of people so you can be all over the news. So where's the best place to go shoot all these people? Obviously, someplace where nobody can shoot back.

In all honesty I have zero respect for anybody who believes gun-free zones actually work. You are going to commit several hundred felonies, up to and including mass murder, and yet you're going to refrain because there is a *sign?* That No Guns Allowed sign is not a cross that wards off vampires. It is wishful thinking, and really pathetic wishful thinking at that.

The only people who obey No Guns signs are people who obey the law. People who obey the law aren't going on killing sprees.

I once testified before a committee of the Utah State Legislature about the University of Utah's gun ban shortly after the Trolley Square shooting in Salt Lake City. Another disaffected loser scumbag started shooting up this mall. He killed several innocent people before he was engaged by an off-duty police officer who just happened to be there shopping. The off-duty Ogden cop engaged and pinned down the shooter until two responding officers from the SLCPD came up from behind and killed him.[2]

The morning before I testified, I sent one of my employees down to Trolley Square to take a picture of the shopping center's front doors. I then showed that picture to the legislators. One of the listed rules was NO GUNS ALLOWED.

For this argument, by gun-free zones, I don't just mean federally mandated things like the Gun-Free School Zones Act or the state equivalents, but also private instances, like companies forbidding their employees from being armed at work, or stores that put up signs saying, "No Guns Allowed." Either way they're stupid.

Research by economist John Lott puts the percentage of mass killings that take place in gun-free zones at 98 percent.[3]

In a pathetic attempt to refute this, the anti-gun lobbying group Everytown for Gun Safety did a study that claimed only 13 percent of mass shootings take place in gun-free zones.[4] In order to reach this goofy conclusion, they had to tweak the definition of *mass shooting* to *all of them*. We've already been over why that's a blatant lie. The vultures do the same thing when they want to scare people with an artificially inflated count of "school shootings" by including things like someone committing suicide across the street from a school parking lot, in the middle of the night, during the summer.[5]

To distort their denominator of gun-free zones, they include murders inside private residences.[6] Clearly, when you think of gun-free zones, you're thinking about public places that the public can actually walk into, not things like strangers' homes or nuclear power plants, where I've got no expectation that I can enter just because I feel like it, with or without a firearm.

These dishonest sorts also like to say things like, *Fort Hood or the Washington Navy Yard shootings don't count as gun-free zones because clearly the military has guns!* Yeah...locked in a distant armory, while all the regular people working around the base are disarmed. Military bases are throw-the-book-at-you gun-free zones, with responding MPs being no different than responding cops in the outside world.

Disingenuous activists aside, it is clear the overwhelming majority of these events take place where regular people are supposed to be disarmed. When I did a deep dive on this topic back in 2012, I was hard pressed to find any event outside of a gun-free zone where an aggressor had managed to shoot more than a couple people besides the Gabby Giffords shooting in Tucson. And that nut's manifesto was so bizarre that he was hearing colors, so I don't know how much forethought he put into his tactics.[7]

So gun-free zones are clearly the preferred target of aspiring mass murderers. That's a no-brainer. But what about regular criminals, who are just doing the usual rape, robbery, and occasional murder sort of thing? Surely, they'll obey those No Gun signs, right?

Or more likely those signs just tell them the best places to do crime without worrying about getting shot. If I'm going to attack or rob somebody, do I go to Big Chuck's Shooting Range & Pit Bull Adoption Center or the Feminist Bookstore & Healing Crystal Emporium with the No Guns Allowed signs stuck all over it? Sure, that's a pretty extreme example, and sometimes there is an armed robber dumb enough to try Big Chuck's, but the security camera videos that end up on YouTube afterwards are hilarious.

Gun-free zones in businesses are the product of nervous HR departments and activist busybodies. They serve no actual point, and then when bad things happen, they directly contribute to the body count. Remember, the single best way to stop an active shooter is by an immediate, violent response. Gun-free zones guarantee that process will take longer.

Another added problem with no-guns-at-work policies is that they artificially limit where working people concealed carry everywhere else. If you've got a permit—or live in a constitutional carry state—and you'd like to lawfully have a gun on your person to protect yourself, but it is against your company policy to have one at work and you don't want to get fired, you are left with a few bad choices.

If you wear your handgun to work and then leave it in your car, that requires taking a weapon off your person and stowing it, which is an unnecessary manipulation of a loaded weapon in an awkward place, which creates a needless danger of a negligent discharge. Worse, guns left in cars tend to get stolen. Repeatedly I've talked about how most guns used by criminals are stolen, and the most common way to steal them is from a vehicle. The reason people with CCWs take their guns off and leave them in their cars is because they have to enter a gun-free zone.

The other option for our law-abiding citizen who has to do business in a gun-free zone is to just leave his gun home. Then he's disarmed not only at work, but also on his commute, and all the locations where he might have errands on the way home. All of which are places he might need a gun. Oh well. When he gets murdered by a tweaker on a meth-fueled psychotic break while out on his lunch hour, I'm sure his company's HR department will send his widow flowers.

When I was teaching CCW, I would constantly urge my students to carry all the time, whenever it was legally possible, and make that a habit. That way if/when that terrible moment arrives and you really need your gun, it isn't sitting in your safe at home. Yet the biggest single reason people gave me for not carrying was their jobs banned it. Since most people spend such a big chunk of their lives at work, or going to and from work, they never get into that habit, so they're disarmed everywhere else.

Gun-free businesses and government buildings mess with a legally armed public. If permit holders honor the signs (which are legally binding in some states), they now have to stow their weapons before entering. Sure, they could just let these people come in and do their business and leave like everybody else, and nobody would ever even know if they were armed or not. But nah, can't have that. Let's have them unnecessarily manipulating loaded firearms in the parking lot and then leave them in their cars to be stolen.

The people who put these policies into place are usually motivated by ignorance, fear, or an outright hostility toward gun rights. For that last group, the process is the punishment. They don't care if you get murdered as long as they get to bully you beforehand. They will put up every roadblock they can to keep you from exercising your rights, just out of spite.

Now, what do we do about this?

Push back. If your state has created some ridiculous gun-free zones, contact your state legislators about them. Get involved with your state-level gun rights organizations. At your job, agitate for change. Be cool about this and don't do it in a way that's going to get you fired. Every company's culture is different. For those of you reading this who are in management, quit being the problem.

If you were going to shop at a business that forbids concealed carry, make sure they know why you're taking your business to their competitors.

I've seen proposals for laws to make employers or property owners liable for injuries that occur because their employees or guests were disarmed. Gun-free zones are not created equal. There is a difference between a secure facility with fences, metal detectors, and armed guards versus your office building that has a glass door and a plastic sign featuring a picture of a gun with a slash through it. By not letting you have access to proper tools to defend yourself, they should be taking on responsibility for your safety. If a maniac decides to murder you there, he's not going to care about HR's feelings.

Most importantly, don't be an idiot. If you are carrying a firearm in public, do so discreetly and safely. Concealed means concealed. Keep it secured, on your person, in a quality holster. Don't be like the moronic Capitol Police officer who left his duty gun in the bathroom.[8] Some gun-free zones exist because some dope was screwing around with his gun when he shouldn't have and frightened the HR department. Don't be that guy.

Gun-free zones need to go. They're not just a failure, they are a solution that actively costs lives.

Stop the Social Contagion

Not all mass killers are the same.

Some of them are ideologically driven. Some have a political or religious motive. There are terrorists on a mission, and others who are just delusional and bug-nuts crazy, with no motive that any sane person can make sense of. However there is one subset that shares some commonalities. These are the disaffected, alienated, angry young men. They usually see themselves as victims and are striking back at whomever they feel has wronged them. That might be their peers at school, some specific group they despise, or just society in general.

These killers want to make a statement. They want to show the world that they aren't losers. They want to make us understand their pain. They want to make the rest of us realize that they are powerful. They'll show us.

It's uncomfortable, but put yourself in their shoes for a minute. They're evil, but they're not an incomprehensible evil. The ones who end up in jail rather than dead are often happy to talk about why they did what they did. Pretend you're one of these men.

You think your life sucks and it's somebody else's fault. You've had a rotten childhood. Your existence has no meaning. Days pass in futile, lonely desperation. Your relationships have fallen apart. Everyone hates you and you hate them. You despise the world.

So you've decided to hurt them back. Make them pay attention. But how?

The solution is easy. It's right there in front of your nose.

Your entire life you have been taught that if you can kill enough people at one time, your picture will be plastered all over the TV and internet, twenty-four seven, round-the-clock coverage. You will become the most famous person in the world. Everyone will know your name. You will be a celebrity. Experts will try to understand what you were thinking. The President of the United States, the most powerful man on Earth, will drop whatever he is doing and hold a press conference to talk about your actions, and he'll even tear up and cry about what you've done.

You are a star.

Hell, they'll literally put your face on *Rolling Stone*, just like a rock star. You want to get your words out there? People are gonna pay attention now. Make that YouTube video. Write that manifesto. Oh, they're going to read it for sure now! Yeah, deep down you know this is probably a one-way trip, but life sucks, and you've been thinking about ending it all anyway, and maybe you've even tried. Might as well buy that ticket and take the ride, because it's better to flame out than fade away. And for a few days you get to be more famous than God.

So now you start to plan.

If you're smart enough, you notice some killers get to be more famous than others. It's pretty obvious what the news and the influencers like to talk about, so you might as well give it to them. People are jaded. They need a high body count. The more corpses, the more clicks. Obviously that means going someplace your victims can't fight back. The last thing you want to do is get shot by some random putz right out the gate, because then you're not going to get on TV at all.

The news has shown you the best kinds of victims. The younger and more helpless the better. Plus you hated school anyway. The only reason to hit something else is if you hate that thing more, like church, or your stupid job. But if you don't really care, hit something with some symbolism, like a holiday parade. The news ghouls love that stuff.

The media is so helpful they even taught you what kind of gun to use. The news talks about how super deadly an AR-15 is, so that should be perfect. If you've got a clean record, and most of you do, you can just go buy one. But if you've got a record and can't pass a background check, just steal one. They're the most common gun in the country now, so it's not like it's going to be hard to find one for you to take. So if you use one of those guns, the media will reward you with *extra* coverage. Make sure to take a selfie posing with the murder weapon beforehand, because that guarantees all the blue checks on Twitter will share your pic everywhere.

And then the cycle repeats, as the next disaffected angry loner takes notes.

■   ■   ■

Our news media directly contributes to cultivating mass killers. They're recruiters.

Strangely enough, this is one of the only topics I actually agreed with Roger Ebert on. He didn't think that the news should pay any attention to the shooters or mention their names on the front page of the paper.[9] But whenever the press isn't talking about guns, or violent movies, or violent video games, or any other thing that hundreds of millions of people enjoyed yesterday without murdering anybody, they'll keep showing the killer's picture in the background while telling the world all about him and his struggles.

Killers should not be glamorized. They should be hated, despised, and forgotten. They are not victims. They are not powerful. They are murdering scum, and the only time their names should be mentioned is when decent people are studying the tactics of how to neutralize them faster.

Instead our system has developed a sick, symbiotic relationship with mass murderers. The killers get the fame and validation they desire, and the news gets ratings and websites get clicks. Afterwards the gun control politicians come along and reap the harvest.

It's a social contagion. The spontaneous spreading of ideas. If you're a listless loser with a meaningless life thinking about punching your own ticket, do it this way and you can die famous. If this idea is not being spread on purpose, the media is so effective at it they might as well be. The news doesn't care though. They have to realize their breathless, panicked, round-the-clock coverage of mass killers bestows instant celebrity, but they keep doing it anyway.

Note, I've gone through this entire book and never once used the names of any of these killers. If I need to talk about a specific example, I use the place they terrorized. Not them. Remember the victims. Let the killers rot in prison or hell, their names forgotten.

Members of the media don't just enable these killers to reach their goals, they provide a road map for how to maximize their fame. All the killers have to do is watch what they fixate on, and then give them more of that. If the media likes to report on a certain kind of target getting hit, hit that kind of target. And if you really want to get coverage, make sure you use whatever specific kind of gun they really want to ban this year. We've had killers write in their manifestos how their target and weapon selection was designed to garner maximum media attention. The racist trash who went on a rampage in Buffalo wrote in his manifesto about how he loved New York's gun laws because it was doubtful anybody would be able to shoot back.[10] Some killers have recorded their crimes because they know the media will air the footage, as some vapid announcer warns the audience beforehand about the shocking scenes of carnage not suitable for young viewers.

On the off chance there's an honest reporter reading this (I won't get my hopes up), stop and examine what you're doing. Ask your people why are we giving these evil bastards exactly what they desire? Why are we motivating the next killer? Clicks? Ratings? To help your team get elected? Then when you see the next manifesto saying he killed a bunch of people exactly how you wanted him to, you should ask yourself if it was worth it.

Trust in American media companies has collapsed, and for good reason. They're scum. They deserve to fail. Let's help them fail faster. This isn't a First Amendment issue either. I'm not asking for any legislation telling journalists what they can and can't say. They have a right to be opportunistic trash, but we've got the right to mock them. Don't be afraid to be honest. We're way past the point of politeness. Make sure all your low-information friends understand what they're doing. Stop watching news that gives the killers what they want. Don't give in to clickbait. You don't need to see the killer's glossy headshots and hear about their stupid philosophies to know about their crimes.

As long as the media is rewarding mass killers, we need to stop rewarding the media.

Push for a Hearing Protection Act

This is a potential law that gets talked about whenever Republicans are trying to get gun owners motivated to vote and then abandoned once they don't need us anymore. Spineless politicians aside, a Hearing Protection Act would be a great thing to have. Basically this would mean making sound suppressors for firearms easier to own. The hang-up is that this idea scares the heck out of people who learned everything they know about guns from action movies and cop shows.

Education time. How do suppressors work and why do we use them?

When a cartridge is fired, the gun powder burns extremely rapidly, and this creates pressure that forces the bullet down the barrel. When those hot expanding gasses escape into the atmosphere, it is rather energetic and extremely loud. That's the bang.

If you've ever been around a really loud noise, you may have noticed that afterwards your ears ring. I've got some bad news for you, that ringing means you've permanently damaged your hearing. When that fades you will have lost some measure of hearing, and hearing damage is permanent and cumulative. The more of these loud noises you are exposed to, the greater the damage. It will never get better. It will only continue to get worse.

When you are shooting for training, practice, or fun, you wear earplugs or earmuffs. For self-defense purposes you probably aren't going to have the time to put hearing protection in, but in that case getting some hearing damage is a reasonable trade-off to keep from getting murdered.

I've spent a lot of time shooting, running ranges, and teaching people. During this I have always been religious about wearing my hearing protection, but if you spend enough time on the range, you will be caught unaware eventually and somebody is going to touch something off right after you take your muffs off.

I have tinnitus. Basically, there is literally no sound of silence in my world. For me it is a constant ringing noise that's about the same pitch as lawn sprinklers. I also can't pick up a lot of sounds in higher pitches, like for many years, my young daughters' voices. If you ever speak to me in a crowded place, you'll notice that I tend to lean way in to get closer to the speaker. That's not because I'm being weird, it's that I can't understand you, especially in a room with background noise that aggravates the perpetual ringing.

I'm not alone. I'm sure audiologists love old gun nuts because they sell a lot of hearing aids that way.

Guns are loud, but incredibly useful. If you want to be proficient with a firearm, you must train with it. Practice is an absolute necessity, and the more you do it, the better you will shoot under pressure. So we put up with the noise and put things in or over our ears in order to mitigate the damage as much as possible.

However, muffs slip. It is really easy to break the seal on an ear-muff when you place your cheek on the stock of a rifle. Boom. Hearing damage. Or that little foam plug in your ear isn't squished in quite right, or deforms and falls out? Boom. Hearing damage. I used to hate when I came home from a long day teaching a class and I'd hear that ring that told me that at some point I'd screwed up. Because there's no going back.

Suppressors were invented to mitigate that danger. You can call them silencers too, that's fine. "Silencer" was basically a brand name—not a particularly accurate description—that's just what Hiram Percy Maxim called suppressors when he invented them a long time ago.[11] It's like Xerox or Kleenex. Many of us gun nuts just refer to them as cans, because that's essentially all they are.

Firearms suppressors work like the muffler on your car. As those expanding gasses from the burning gunpowder escape the muzzle, instead of all that flying outward to bombard those delicate little hairs in your ears, the gasses are trapped in a can screwed onto the end. It leaks out slower instead of blasting out fast. That's basically all they're doing.

Suppressors are usually filled with something that increases the interior surface area that gives that energy more things to bounce off of. In the olden days we used things like rubber gaskets, steel wool, grease, and all sorts of other stuff. Nowadays, because of good precision machining, they use metal baffles. The hardest part about building a can to last is dealing with the temperature. The energy that would normally escape as noise gets trapped as heat. Cans get hot fast.

When you screw a suppressor onto the end of your gun, it isn't usually going to make it silent. Not even close. The actual noise reduction is going to vary greatly depending on a whole bunch of different factors. The size, quality, and construction of the can is secondary to the power level of the gun. The more powerful the boom, the more can required to contain it. It's all about the amount of expanding gasses escaping that muzzle. The other downside of suppressors is that they are adding some cumbersome length and weight to the end of your gun.

Also, most bullets are supersonic. Just like a fighter jet, as that bullet breaks the speed of sound it is going to make a sonic boom. Though since bullets are much smaller, it is more of a sonic *crack*. The baffles in a modern can never actually touch the bullet, so they do nothing about the bullet breaking the sound barrier.

I won't get into decibel ratings—which are indecipherable gibberish to most folks anyway—but if you slap a suppressor onto a standard rifle, shooting standard ammunition, it is still fairly loud. It is still noticeable by anybody nearby. Everybody is still going to hear the sonic crack of the bullet.

Only for the shooter it doesn't feel like you're getting hit in the ear canal with a hammer.

Regular pistols with regular ammo aren't movie-gun quiet either. Not even close. In the movies the elite hitman shoots somebody with his 9mm, and other people in the room don't even hear it. In reality a suppressed 115-grain standard 9mm round sounds like taking a big dictionary and slamming it flat on a hardwood floor. *WHUMP.* Bystanders are still going to hear, it's just not as sharp. A 147-grain subsonic 9mm is going to be a little quieter because it won't have the crack. It's more of a *chuff* noise. But John Wick movies aside, everybody nearby is still going to hear it firing.

There's also the mechanical action of the gun working. On a semi-automatic firearm, the action is still going to cycle, and that also makes a pretty distinct metallic noise. Bullet impacts are also surprisingly loud, especially when they land close to you.

There seems to be this misconception that suppressors will make murders go unnoticed. If you're close enough to realize it's a gunshot with a regular gun, you're probably close enough to realize it's a gunshot with a silenced gun. And contrary to popular belief, the cops don't immediately come running to investigate every time there are some loud noises. Have you ever been to a big American city?

Can you get a gun "movie quiet"? Yes. It is possible. However it means using slower, subsonic ammunition that never breaks the sound barrier, a high quality can, and a manually operated firearm like a bolt action. The easiest way to get really quiet is with the common lowly .22 LR, though there are bigger specialty subsonic calibers (not cheap, but fun). All of those are going to be inferior to regular velocity rifle bullets over longer distances because slower bullets will drop more, which means it is harder to hit things further away. In the words of Robert Heinlein, "There ain't no such thing as a free lunch."[12]

Basically, cans aren't magic. All this stuff is just basic physics.

Contrary to what many people think, suppressors are already perfectly legal at the federal level, and legal in most U.S. states right now. They're legal, but pointlessly overregulated.

The law for suppressors dates back to the 1930s (the National Firearms Act) and it doesn't make a lick of sense. The NFA is like the poster child for silly, pointless government inefficiency.

Quick version: In order to purchase a suppressor, you need to get it from a special kind of gun dealer (an SOT Title 3 or 7, like I was). Then you fill out some special federal paperwork (the Form 4) and pay a $200 tax to the ATF. This paperwork is actually pretty simple, the kind of thing that would be processed by a private company in minutes, but ATF usually takes about a YEAR (not a typo) to cash your check, stamp the paper, and mail it back to you, so that you can take possession of your suppressor.

This ridiculous delay varies, and the ATF processes about two million Form 4s per year. For the last can I bought, it took the ATF nine months to approve it. I've had them come back for customers as fast as a couple of months, and as long as eighteen. It's not like they're doing a rigorous background check that whole time or anything. That's all done instantly with a computer database. It is literally just months of waiting for a government employee to work through the stack, stamp your paper, and put it in the registry.

Like I talked about in the Do-Something section about automatic weapons, the $200 tax is a racist relic leftover from 1934, when the government decided that rich people should have more rights than poor people.

A Hearing Protection Act would simply move suppressors from the NFA to treating them like they were regular serialized firearms instead. It would get rid of the tax and the ridiculous time delay. The NFA is bloated, inefficient, slow, and basically a useless relic regulating 1930s-level tech. We have a National Instant Criminal Background Check System already for firearms purchases, so there's no reason they couldn't just use it instead. Personally, I think they're just glorified pipes, so even treating them like a firearm at all is kind of stupid, but it's an improvement over our current archaic system.

The current system is ripe for abuse too, because even though suppressors are legal and common, if you possess one without jumping through the hoops, getting that stamp, and paying the tax, it's a felony with massive penalties (ten years in prison and huge fines). The ATF loves when the gullible or ignorant buy illegal suppressors. There are even ads on Facebook for "fuel filters" that just happen to be the exact right size to screw onto common guns. When my people see those ads we just assume they were placed by feds looking for a dope who doesn't know any better.

Even European countries that have far stricter gun control than the United States don't regulate suppressors like we do. In Europe using a can at a public range is considered polite. They're useful for hunting, because you don't walk through a forest listening for game wearing earplugs. They're also kinder to our pets because hunting dogs can go deaf too.

I love using them for helping kids learn how to shoot. My rifle for teaching first timers is a suppressed .22. There is a lot less distracting noise and no scary muzzle blast, which makes the inexperienced less jumpy, making it easier for them to concentrate on mastering things like safety and basic marksmanship.

However, when you bring up a Hearing Protection Act, the anti-gun zealot crowd reacts as expected. They despise the idea of quieter guns and will of course launch into a bunch of outlandish scenarios based on elite movie hitmen silently picking off guards to get to their target, ninja style. Despite the panicked flailing of the anti-gun zealots, there is nothing stopping a murderer from getting one already, unless you think elite, professional, video-game-style assassins can't afford a $200 tax, or just, you know...can't make, steal, or buy an illegal one like every other kind of criminal in the world.

As for making them at home, they're basically a pipe with some stuff inside of them. Anybody who wants to make one can. Really easily. People have even made them out of oil filters and soda bottles. And as we've covered a great many times, murderers don't give a crap about gun laws. *Oh, I was totally going to whack these rival drug dealers, but that extra NFA violation is just a bridge too far, man!*

In real life suppressors are just another tool to make training safer and more pleasant. They make communicating on the range easier. And truthfully, they're a lot of fun. Every time I let a new shooter try one of mine, they're amazed at how much nicer it is to not get thumped in the ear hole, and when they ask how they can get one, I have to explain all this convoluted nonsense about racist taxes, and how they'll have to wait a year because people who know nothing about guns are scared of movie villains.

It's time to get rid of this pointless regulation. An HPA is a great thing to ask your political candidates about, to test if they are truly pro-gun or just paying lip service to the idea to get your votes.

Remove Short Barrels from the NFA

Back when I used to work at gun shows, my employees and I would always bring the *emergency* tool kit with us. This was useful for setting up our displays, but the reason it was called the emergency kit was that it also came in handy whenever I'd see some unsuspecting schlub walking around in the crowd, inadvertently carrying an illegal gun, totally unaware that he was committing a felony. This was usually some young dude who simply didn't know any better, who had just stuck some parts on his gun because he thought they looked cool. These poor saps usually had no idea that sticking a couple pieces of otherwise innocuous plastic together could ruin their lives.

So I'd get the guy's attention and quietly ask, "Hey, dude, you got a tax stamp for that?"

And he'd go, "What's a tax stamp?"

Oh boy. Here we go. And rather than explain all the convoluted legal nonsense I'm about to go over in this section, I'd grab the emergency tool kit and tell the kid, "You've assembled an illegal SBR/AOW, and this crowd is filled with undercover ATF agents and their criminal informants, so unless you want to go to prison for ten years, you're gonna want to unscrew that grip/stock right now."

If he went, "Oh crap!" and started disassembling his illegal gun, I knew he was a normal person. If he blew off my warning and kept walking, that told me he was the CI, and he was there looking to sell that felony to some unsuspecting dupe in the crowd.

We once again return to the National Firearms Act of 1934 for another pointless regulation, and this section is so awful that it has created the potential for the ATF to make *millions* of gun owners felons overnight, because they bought something that was perfectly legal... until some bureaucrat decided it wasn't.

In addition to regulating machine guns and suppressors, the NFA also covered "short-barreled" rifles (SBR) and shotguns (SBS). Rifle barrels need to be over sixteen inches, shotguns over eighteen, and both need to have an overall length of twenty-six inches. Anything below that is subject to the NFA. Just like suppressors, you can still get one legally, but you have to go through that same ridiculous process of paperwork, $200 tax, and the pointless waiting for your stamp to come back.

I believe the goal behind this was to keep rifles and shotguns from being "concealable," which was frankly impossible since coats had already been invented.

And once again, since criminals don't care about laws, if they want their shotgun—probably stolen anyway—to be shorter, they just take a hacksaw to it. I once got to tour a state crime lab and see the room where they kept all the evidence guns seized from criminals. There were hundreds and hundreds of regular old wood-and-blue-steel hunting guns that somebody had roughly sawed the stocks or barrels off of. It's not like this is rocket science. It's gunsmithing so easy you can do it on meth!

Meanwhile, regular people love short-barreled rifles and shotguns because they're really useful in some circumstances. They're lighter, handier, and easier to maneuver in cramped surroundings. Many guns, especially those originally designed in foreign countries, were never intended to have a barrel that long, so the versions imported into America with sixteen-inch barrels look ridiculous and handle like garbage.

The light and handy part is especially helpful for people who have physical disabilities that impair their upper body strength or mobility. Leave it to the government to come up with a law that actively punishes the elderly and handicapped.

In the last section, I talked about how useful suppressors are, but one of the downsides is the extra length and weight. Pairing a suppressor with a short barrel gets you a rifle that's a reasonable length to use and won't cause you hearing damage. Too bad you now have to get two tax stamps and pay $400 to ask the crown for that privilege.

As usual, criminals don't care, while the law abiding get restricted. This may sound a lot like the same issues we talked about for suppressors in the last section, but now we're going to go over how the law for short-barreled guns gets *really weird*. This next part will probably confuse you, but don't feel bad. This stuff confuses everybody, especially the federal agents in charge of enforcing it.

One thing to note, because this will be very important later, is that pistols normally don't have stocks, and rifles and shotguns usually do. The stock is the part that you press against your shoulder for added stability and recoil control. Guns with stocks tend to be a lot easier to control and shoot accurately than guns without. This makes sense to everybody but Congress.

Now on to the goofy part...

If you have a pistol, and you put a stock on it, that is an NFA violation because you are creating an illegal SBR. If you take an existing rifle and you cut the barrel below sixteen inches, you've created an illegal SBR. Big fines and prison time.

However, if you take that exact same model of rifle, only you build it with a barrel shorter than sixteen inches, and it's got no stock, legally that's a *pistol*...However, if you put a stock on this "pistol" you've now created an illegal SBR, and the ATF will come to your house and shoot your dog. If you screw a vertical fore grip on this "pistol" you've now created an illegal AOW (Any Other Weapon), which may also result in prison terms and repeated showings of *All Dogs Go to Heaven.*

What possible crime were they trying to prevent when they made it illegal to put a vertical grip on the front of a pistol? I honestly have no idea, but I don't think Congress did either when they wrote it.

But wait...there's more!

Whenever an enterprising gun designer comes up with something truly new, they have to send it to the ATF for testing and approval. The ATF then issues a ruling on whether this new invention complies with the NFA or not.

In 2012 a company (SB Tactical) submitted a design for a "stabilizing brace" to the ATF. This was emphatically *not* a shoulder stock. It was shaped sort of like a stock and mounted where stocks usually mount, but it was intended to be braced against the shooter's arm, not his shoulder. Which would theoretically not violate the NFA because it wasn't adding a stock to a pistol.[12]

And the ATF said, *Okay. It's not a stock. You can sell it.*

Immediately all of us gun nuts were like, *Wait, what? You're sure? Because you guys have a history of shooting people for possessing shotgun barrels that are an eighth of an inch too short. You're sure you're sure? Okay then*...Then we promptly started buying *millions* of short-barreled "pistols" with braces, that just happened to look and function a whole lot like our SBRs, only without having to write a check for $200 and then waiting a year for the ATF to get around to cashing it so we could take our gun home.

This was perfectly legal according to the ATF's own decree. Until a couple years later when the ATF realized that law-abiding American gun owners were having fun wrong and tried to *clarify* its ruling.

Braces were legal, as long as you only used them against your arm, but if you put them against your shoulder you were creating an illegal SBR. Yes. The ATF actually tried to say that *holding something wrong* was a felony.

This of course led to legal battles, because moving your hands four more inches shouldn't be considered *manufacturing an illegal firearm*. The ATF backed down, then came back to try again, and then backed down, and is basically still blundering around in a holding pattern.

Meanwhile gun owners spent the last decade buying a ludicrous number of brace pistols. I can't even begin to estimate how many of these are now in circulation, but they are extremely popular and now super common.

In 2020 the ATF issued a new proposal that would recategorize all of those brace pistols as NFA items, but then held off when they were met with overwhelming public backlash and criticism. It turns out that millions of Americans didn't like the idea of being turned into felons by the stroke of a pen. However, this is still out there pending, and Joe Biden recently talked about making stabilizing braces illegal as part of his gun control wish list.[13]

But what's the point? For almost ninety years these things have been heavily regulated, and it made no difference to criminals. For the last ten years, Americans found a perfectly legal work-around, ran with it, and it made no difference to criminals, who just kept on doing their thing either way.

The ugly truth is gun control zealots don't care about stopping crime, any more than criminals care about breaking laws. It is about bossing around the little people they hate, like me and you.

To illustrate how absurd this is, recently a Florida man, who was a former police dispatcher with no criminal record, who had passed a background check to get a CCW, and who had already gone through the NFA process *twice* previously, was sent to prison for manufacturing an illegal short-barreled rifle. All he did was take an existing gun and attach a stock to it, and he only ever used it on his own private property.

If he had stuck a nearly identical-looking stabilizing brace to it instead, that would have been legal. The best part was, in order to bust this dangerous menace to society for committing this victimless crime of putting the slightly different-looking piece of plastic on another piece of plastic, all it took was a three-month-long sting operation involving an FBI informant wearing a hidden camera.[14]

I've talked about the recent Supreme Court decision relating to the Second Amendment, *New York State Rifle & Pistol Association, Inc. v. Bruen*, but there was another decision that same week that I think should pertain to the ATF's inane back-and-forth on braces, and that was *West Virginia v. EPA*. Basically SCOTUS said that making laws is Congress's job, and federal agencies just can't make up rules out of thin air and expect everyone to obey them. Making up rules out of thin air is the ATF's second favorite thing, after shooting pets, so you can see where I'm going with this. This is the same agency that once declared a shoelace with a loop tied on each end to be an illegal machine gun.[15]

Between court challenges and the sheer mass of brace purchasers rendering the SBR rules irrelevant, I've got hope that we can get rid of this egregiously dumb part of a very dumb law.

However, none of this would matter if we could just end the NFA entirely.

End the NFA Entirely

Yes. I'm going to go there. I might offend some of you, but I'll argue for legal machine guns. I know this is very unlikely to happen anytime soon, and is a very big reach, but it needs to be considered, because at its base the law as it stands now is just as illogical and fear based as every other gun control law.

We've already discussed the other things the National Firearms Act covers. There's no point to their suppressor or short-barrel rules. The other part is for weird things like "Any Other Weapons," and there hasn't been a rash of murders involving umbrella guns, so I'm not going to worry about those. So we've established that all the other provisions of the NFA are hot garbage, and the whole tax thing is rooted in racism and classism, in the elites' attempt to keep scary guns out of the hands of the unworthy poors.

We've already talked about how new automatic weapons were available clear into the 1980s, and though there haven't been any new ones manufactured for sale to regular people since 1986, the ones already in existence remain legal to own and transfer, and almost none of those have ever been used in a crime. Which is pretty cool considering that between pre-1986 transferable machine guns and post-1986 dealer samples, there are about half a million legal machine guns already in the hands of regular citizens in the United States.[16]

However, illegal machine guns still turn up in the U.S., usually in gang or drug crime, because, as usual, criminals don't care about gun laws. If you're going to go back to prison for possession of any gun, might as well make it a fun one. It is not that difficult to convert an existing semi-auto—the most common type of gun in the country—to full-auto. And if you are building a gun from scratch, full-auto is actually simpler to make. (It's more complicated to make it stop than to make it go.) We have an active drug trade across our giant border, moving tons of drugs and hundreds of thousands of people every year, run by cartels who are better equipped than the Mexican army—or in some cases equipped *by* the Mexican army—yet we're supposed to believe that if a hardened criminal really wants something full-auto that it's going to be difficult for him to get?

Even then machine guns are rarely used as murder weapons. By far the most common guns used in crime are regular old handguns, for the same reasons handguns are the most common guns used in legal self-defense: portability and accessibility. Not that a criminal can't convert a normal concealable pistol to full-auto, but doing so makes it really hard to control. The cyclic rate is extremely fast, and unless the shooter has got a lot of practice, he's going to dump most of his mag somewhere above the target or into the ceiling.

But what about mass killers? Won't they be even deadlier if they've got a full-auto? Well, there's not really much stopping them from using an illegal machine gun if they wanted to. Keeping in mind these kinds of events are already anomalous to begin with, it's impossible to predict an outcome because it depends on what the circumstances of your hypothetical situation are. However, to get any extra utility out of an automatic weapon requires a lot more skill than the usual untrained disaffected losers we see. They'd expend their ammo faster and have to reload more often, but would they actually hit more people? Depends, but doubtful.

Standard issue for the U.S. military is the M-4 carbine. Even though it is capable of full-auto fire, it's almost always used for rapid, aimed, *semi-auto* fire, because that's by far the best way to get accurate hits. In military usage full-auto is usually reserved for belt-feds. A machine gunner's job is different than a regular rifleman. They're the base of fire for a squad. They lay down fire to keep the enemy's heads down so the rest of the squad can maneuver. They're larger, much heavier guns, with a bigger ammo supply on tap.

So you might be thinking, if full-auto is more challenging to use, and it's got all these drawbacks, why do I want the NFA repealed so regular citizens can buy new legal machine guns again?

Because you either believe the Second Amendment is necessary for the security of a free state and our rights should not be infringed...or you don't.

Personally I do. Which means that the guns we choose to own shouldn't be any of the government's damn business.

I had easy access to machine guns when I worked in the gun business. Did I suddenly become less of a citizen simply because I changed careers? Why are my constitutional rights dependent upon what licensing fees I pay to a government agency?

The only way I see the entirety of the NFA being repealed is through the courts. All the nominally pro-gun politicians will run from this one, and the zealots will have a total apocalyptic come-apart. However, the last two SCOTUS decisions on this topic have confirmed the Second Amendment means what it says, and that includes weapons that are common and have clear use in a militia sense. It's pretty hard to argue that the most common type of military small arm doesn't have a militia application.

■   ■   ■

One further note on the NFA related to machine guns. Bump stocks are *not* full-auto. They simply don't fit the legal definition at all. Machine guns are self-loading firearms, where the gun keeps firing as long as the trigger is depressed or it runs out of ammo. Bump stocks don't do that. They're spring loaded and bounce a semi-auto rifle back and forth under recoil. The shooter is still firing one shot per trigger pull, but the recoil is resetting the trigger back against the shooter's finger faster. That's it.

However, this did not stop Trump's ATF from declaring them to be illegal machine guns, even though Congress never passed any laws outlawing what bump stocks actually do. People who bought a legal product found themselves in possession of a felony.

The other type of item that gets rolled up in this is what's called a forced reset trigger. Forced reset triggers achieve an effect sort of like a bump stock, where in semi-auto the trigger is reset faster, so it can get pulled again faster. Since it is still the user's finger pulling the trigger separately each time, these clearly don't fit the legal definition either. Except that hasn't stopped the ATF from changing its mind and making up rules again.

Personally I'm not a fan of bump stocks. I think they're a silly gimmick, but that's beside the point that this is ridiculous government overreach, and federal agencies shouldn't be able to just make up laws out of thin air to screw people over. This is another example of why the NFA needs to go.

Make State Laws Fall Like Dominos

Whether by legislation or through the courts, this one is happening now, and I hope to see it accelerate.

What each of us can do personally for this one will depend on what state we live in, with some states being fanatically dedicated to stomping on gun rights at every opportunity. I have nothing but respect for the Californian gun owners who've been bashing their heads against that brick wall. But even gun-friendly states often retain some goofy laws that need to go. Expanding gun ownership and easy, common CCW makes it harder for state legislatures to cling to unpopular, pointless regulations, while the recent *New York State Rifle & Pistol Association, Inc. v. Bruen* decision opens up all-new avenues for residents of states with draconian laws to sue to get their rights back.

After the *Bruen* ruling was handed down, the Supreme Court remanded four cases back to the lower courts to reexamine in light of their decision. These include challenges to Maryland's assault weapons ban, Hawaii's ban on open carry, and California and New Jersey laws banning magazines that hold more than ten rounds.[17] By the clear logic of the ruling, all of these laws should be found unconstitutional and void.

However, it took a long time to accumulate the mountain of dumb gun laws we have now, so it will take a while to chip all of them away. It's frustrating, but we didn't get here overnight. Obstinate governors will fight loosening gun laws tooth and nail, and we've seen that as one type of draconian control scheme gets slapped down, they're quick to switch to a new one. Immediately after *Bruen* declared New York's may issue concealed carry law to be unconstitutional, New York's proposed replacement was just as ridiculous but in a different way, with the state requiring from the applicant three years of his social media history to check for "good character."[18]

Yep. Your memes are too spicy. No Second Amendment rights for you.

I'm lucky I don't live in New York, because I've hurt a lot of people's feelings on the internet.

How can you help improve your state laws?

Get involved in your local politics. Your primaries are the best chance to pick pro-gun candidates. I can tell some of you are rolling your eyes right now, and, depending on your state, I'm totally naïve and that's not going to happen. If everything is broken or lopsided where you live, you're probably right, but for the people who live in states with governments that don't resemble a Third World junta, this is still useful.

Get your friends involved. Gun ownership should be a right valued by every American who doesn't want to be a victim.

It is easy for people to underestimate how much clout they have in state-level politics. They say all politics are local, but when your state legislator only represents a few thousand people, and most of them don't show up, you can actually be heard. If he won't listen, you can help replace him next time. I don't know how many times there has been a massive push in a state for some new anti-gun legislation, and the media is all in on promoting it, and all the proper, important people support it, so it seems like a done deal...until the motivated gun owners turn out in huge numbers to say, *Oh hell no*!

Join your local state-level gun rights organizations. They—hopefully—are the people who have their fingers on the pulse of your state's legislative possibilities. I say hopefully because in my experience the quality between different state level orgs can vary greatly, from fantastic to abysmal. But hey, if they're abysmal, maybe you're just the kind of volunteer they need to help improve it? If you're not a joiner, I respect that, but at least sign up for their newsletter so you can keep up on pending legislation.

There are several national-level gun rights orgs, and where they really help at the state level is joining and funding lawsuits. The Firearms Policy Coalition, Second Amendment Foundation, and the NRA's Institute for Legislative Action do this, and it is fantastic. Look into them, and, if you've got the money, donate to whomever you think is doing good work.

Be the Best Gun Owner You Can Be

I'm not going to blow smoke about your being a brand ambassador or anything so trite, but let's be honest. A lot of the dumb stereotypes about gun owners exist for a reason. Some jackass somewhere did something stupid, so that's going to be used to smear all of us.

Now obviously when we're dealing with a profoundly dishonest media, if there's not something awful they can use, they'll just make something up, but let's not make their job easy for them.

When you're using firearms, conduct yourself responsibly.

I'm not talking about the four basic safety rules. That's a given. Those are always in effect. I'm talking about the ancillary stuff.

If you are shooting on public lands, clean up after yourself. When some dork leaves his trashed targets all over the ground, it makes all of us look bad. We're trying to sway voters, not piss them off by leaving shot-up washing machines in the desert. Clean up your crap.

While you are doing gun stuff, be courteous to others. This should be a no-brainer, but some people's parents did a crappy job. Don't let your ego outrun your capabilities.

This next part might be controversial to some gun owners, but let's talk about open carry. By that I mean carrying a firearm openly on your person, either a handgun or a long gun, in public places, around other people. This is legal in quite a few states.

I'm not a big fan of open carry in general. Don't get me wrong. I think it is your right to do so, and sometimes it is appropriate and makes sense. I also believe that it is context specific. In some environments open carry is socially acceptable and most of the people around you are totally cool with it. If you're in a rural area, the woods, or at a gun rights rally, awesome. A lot of other places, you're going to look like a dork who is trying too hard.

There's open carry, and then there's open carrying *at* people. A holstered handgun is one thing, but the guys who open carry a slung AR to shop at Walmart might think they're helping, but they're not. I've heard people say this is making a political statement, and they're *normalizing* guns. No. Really, you're not. Depending on the location it comes off as cringy plea for attention.

When I see somebody openly carrying a long gun in a crowded urban environment that's not a gun-culture-friendly sort of establishment, I usually just quietly and unobtrusively watch for a bit to see if he's a nut who is about to do something bad, or if he's just some doofus who thinks grocery shopping with a rifle makes him look like a badass. That's my reaction and I'm a jaded former machine-gun dealer who writes gun books for a living, so I bet they're making a great impression on those soccer mom swing voters.

As far as open carrying a handgun when you're just going about your business around strangers, why? I've seen some people say it is for *deterrence*...Sure, for one specific type of criminal, but predators are not created equal. For an actual bloodthirsty maniac, it's just a sign that says, *Shoot me first*. Tactically speaking I don't want a bad guy to know who is armed and needs to be taken out priority. Also, though you might think you've got super-awesome around-the-clock situational awareness, if you let your guard down around an opportunistic criminal who can throw a good sucker punch, *Hey, free gun*.

But if you're going to ignore that risk and open carry a handgun, for the love of God, at least do it with a quality holster. If you shove your Taurus in your sweatpants, you've got a 99 percent chance somebody is going to take a picture of you and stick it on the internet to get laughed at. Have some dignity.

On a more serious note, there is another type of carry that I am adamantly against for safety reasons, and that's off the body carry. That's carrying a concealed weapon, but not attached to your body. I'm specifically talking about things like carrying a handgun in a purse or briefcase.

Tactically speaking, it's a stupid way to carry because, ladies, if somebody is going to rob you, what's the first thing he grabs? That's right. Your purse. He's now got more control over your weapon than you do.

But more importantly, if that container ever leaves your side, even for a minute, you have left an unsecured gun unattended in public. This is an accident waiting to happen.

We're in a culture war. Let's not provide ammunition to our enemies.

The Relentless Culture War

The biggest fight for the Second Amendment isn't in Congress, the courts, or state legislatures. It's in the minds of the people.

There is no issue people are more passionate or ignorant about, and that has been capitalized on by anti-gun zealots to peddle nonsense for generations. That's the nature of the battle we face. It's emotion and hyperbole. It's tribal virtue signaling and processes that are the punishment. In an ideal world, gun rights would be a non-partisan, right-and-wrong, logic-versus-illogic, effective-versus-ineffective, constitutional-or-not argument... but that's not how it is, and no amount of wishful thinking will change that.

I've tried to keep this book relatively nonpartisan—at least as much as possible for a topic that's extremely political—but that goes out the window for this section. There's no helping it, because when it comes to defending the Second Amendment there are clear differences between our two main parties. Note, I'm talking about our elected officials, not the rank-and-file voters, because there's often a world of difference between those two groups.

Elected Democrats are universally awful on gun rights. I keep getting told that there are pro-gun Democrats in office, but I've seen more convincing evidence for Bigfoot. At least at the federal level, Democrats tend to be in near perfect lockstep in favor of gun control. Regardless of which of the regular useless Do-Somethings is being proposed, they're all in.

The Republican Party is mediocre on gun rights. There are many reliably pro-gun Republicans in office, some who are ambivalent but not overtly hostile, some actual control freaks who love anything that makes the state more powerful, and then there are the total squishes who are happy to "compromise." And remember, when it comes to guns, compromising always means giving the anti-gun zealots some of what they want while we gain nothing, and whatever we do keep they'll just come back around for later.

You might be thinking, but isn't there a party that's *good* for gun rights? Well, there are third parties who talk a great game, but unless one of them trips over a lamp with a wish-granting genie in it, they're not going to be making a difference in Congress anytime soon.

To illustrate the partisan nature of this issue, in the wake of the Uvalde school shooting—where the police utterly failed in every way imaginable in arguably the most disgusting display of incompetence and cowardice in the history of American law enforcement—the Democrats' immediate reaction was to disarm the regular people to make them count on the state to protect them even more.

Congress passed a wish list of Do-Somethings. *Nearly every single Democrat voted for it.* They were joined by 5 of the 210 Republicans.[19]

In the Senate, which is split fifty-fifty, instead they *compromised* and ended up passing funding for red flag laws. Which also won't work, but not as many voters have caught onto the futility and danger inherent in that particular scam yet. Fifteen of the fifty Republicans voted for this.[20]

As you can see, the elected officials on one side of this debate are reliable, but it's reliably bad. While the other half will probably choke, fail, and let us down when it matters. Some of them are just ruthless pragmatists with zero principles who will do whatever they think will give them the best press coverage, while others are dumb enough to think red flag laws will actually work and not just be gleefully abused by vindictive bullies and nuts. Then there is my senator Mitt Romney, who is such an invertebrate that he's basically a Ziploc bag of hair gel in a human shape.

This "compromise" worked so well that Democrats were satisfied for *two whole weeks* before proposing a new assault weapons ban.[21]

I'm not saying any of this to get you down, but we need to play with the hand we are dealt. As they are currently constituted, the DNC is awful on guns. The GOP is far better, but that's such a low bar that being better than the Democrats isn't exactly a great achievement. There are some stalwart defenders, but they're stuck with whatever coworkers the voters send them.

If we are going to make progress for gun rights, then it is absolutely vital that we not shackle the Second Amendment to any one group, because then it becomes easy for that group to just suck and take our votes for granted. At the individual level, we need to invite everyone, regardless of political affiliation or other beliefs, to enjoy their rights. Self-defense isn't something you should gatekeep with intellectual purity tests.

The reason the ostensibly pro-gun party can be maneuvered into supporting gun control is simple. They think it will benefit them. There's unified pressure from nearly every institution in society to destroy gun rights. This is a direct result of the relentless culture war that's been waged against the very idea of the Second Amendment.

■   ■   ■

The culture war is everywhere and it never ever rests. It's not just about guns, but every other possible topic you can think of. There's a sort of unified theory of goodness that gets shoved down our throats, and it's got no time for nuance. You are either all in favor of topic X or you are the unclean enemy of all that is holy and must be driven from society.

Sadly, even though gun rights should be useful for everyone equally, they have gotten rolled into this too. Half the time when people are arguing against your right to keep and bear arms, they don't actually know or care much, it's just that guns are supposed to belong to the other team, and the other team is always wrong and must be punished.

I'm trying to stay away from all those other political hot buttons on purpose. We're here to talk gun rights. I don't want to offend people who disagree with me about abortion, climate change, taxes, schools, the role of government, or whatever... because the Second Amendment is for them too. All of us have the right to defend our lives, and there is no other tool that's as viable for that as the gun.

We've seen what works, and we've seen what doesn't. Gun rights should be a nonissue at this point that both sides of the political divide just leave be. The anti-gun zealots like to talk about "common sense" gun laws, except the Second Amendment is the "common sense" gun law. It is the baseline.

But we've reached the point where keeping or bearing arms is labeled as *extremism*. Our cultural institutions are united in despising the idea of an armed populace. Hollywood mocks you for wanting to be able to defend yourself, even as they profit off action flicks. Social media banned people for talking about the Rittenhouse case, but only if you came down on the side of saying it was clear-cut self-defense. If you condemned him as a racist murderer (for shooting three white guys?) those posts were fine. And God help you if you say something pro-gun at many of our prestigious universities. Academics are supposed to love debate, but saying you believe in the Second Amendment in school now is more likely to get you red-flagged than tenured.

A reflexive hatred of gun rights is mandatory in certain social circles. It's a wonderful virtue signal that declares you are a proper-thinking member of the good people tribe. When Harvey Weinstein got busted for being a sleazy perverted predator, do you recall what his attempted repentance was? If they'd just allow him to keep making movies, he promised to produce propaganda to destroy the NRA.[22] His attempt at damage control rightfully failed, but his chosen strategy says a lot about the perfidious nature of Hollywood.

Of course, the same movie stars who make emotional music videos after a shooting grabs sufficient headlines live in gated communities and have armed bodyguards. Or they own guns themselves, but that's okay. They're elite. Just like it's been throughout history, control is for the little people.

Politics are downstream of culture. As the institutions set the messages, they are repeated through the masses. It doesn't matter how false or dumb the narrative is, it gets regurgitated. Once a narrative is set, it never goes away. Which is why most "debates" about guns on the internet consist of a wish list of Do-Somethings, followed by the same tired attacks once they get frustrated we don't fold.

"Oh, you want a gun? You must be compensating for your *tiny dick*." Yep. You got me. I'm compensating for the fact my penis is incapable of accurately launching a 115-grain lead projectile at 1100 feet per second, and thus is insufficient for self-defense use.

I'm curious what they think armed women are compensating for? Tiny uteruses? Except the equivalent misogynistic line of attack used by anti-gun zealots against women who stand up for the Second Amendment is usually some variation of "Women shouldn't have a gun because your attacker will just take it away and use it on you."

How disgustingly patronizing is that? That's even dumber than the tiny penis line they use on men. The best response I've seen for this was from gun writer Tamara Keel, who replied to someone saying the bad guy would just take her gun away with, "That's when you pull the Felon Repulsion Lever."

Earlier I talked about the difference between people with genuine questions and the willfully ignorant. You can have a rational discussion with people who are engaging in good faith, but if you are engaging the willfully ignorant, just remember that debate is a spectator sport.

You don't do it expecting to sway your opponent. They exist simply for you to make your case to the audience. If there's no audience, don't waste your time.

And the audience is coming around.

The best thing to break through this team sports mentality is messy, uncomfortable reality, and reality will eventually intrude into even the tidiest little worlds. You can spend your entire life being taught that guns are awful, but there comes a point where it would be super useful to have one. When there is a real threat that no amounts of slogans, dick jokes, or government programs will save you from, it doesn't matter how religiously you listened to NPR, how much you donated to "get guns off our streets," or how faithfully you retweeted the latest outraged screed from a pop star...the cops aren't coming in time.

America has seen endless examples of this over the last few years. Sometimes you're on your own.

And nothing makes you examine your fundamental beliefs quite like the threat of dying for them.

Chapter Seven

The Legalities of Shooting People

Whenever a citizen or a cop shoots somebody and it gets on the news, there is always an avalanche of dumb takes. The more any particular shooting can be twisted to fit a useful political narrative, the harder the media will cram that down our throats. The story they tell—long before the actual facts are known—seldom has any resemblance to reality. They use these cases for emotional manipulation and political gain, and in order to get away with that, they need the populace to remain uneducated about how this stuff actually works.

For most of this book, I've focused on the issues from the perspective of a regular gun owner, not a peace officer, but for this section I'll be talking about police shootings as well, because the same kind of clumsy, dishonest reporting is used to distort both kinds of situations to cause outrage for political gain.

Let's go over the basics of use of force laws.

The laws will vary state to state, but these are the fundamentals that apply to most jurisdictions in the U.S. There are some legal differences between police and regular folks shooting people, but basically the rules are similar. I'm not an attorney, and this is not legal advice in your state. This chapter is a primer to get people to not be so damned ignorant about the fundamentals of how the law works.

And self-defense laws usually do work. After you understand this, you won't be shocked and outraged nearly as often when you hear the ruling come down for some controversial event.

First off you need to understand some terms I'm going to be using.

"Lethal force" is an action taken against someone that may potentially take the person's life. If you shoot somebody and he doesn't die, you still exercised lethal force. If you shoot somebody in the leg or arm, legally that is still lethal force, and contrary to the movies, you can still die if you get shot in the arm or the leg.

"Serious bodily harm" (often called "grievous bodily harm") is any injury that is potentially life altering or life threatening. Rape is serious bodily harm. A beating is serious bodily harm. Anything that may render you unconscious is serious bodily harm.

"Reasonable man." The question isn't whether the shooter perceives himself to be justified, but whether a reasonable man would perceive his decisions to be rational. Contrary to popular opinion, you can't just say, "He was coming right at me!" and be justified in shooting somebody. The evidence will be examined, and the question will be whether or not you made the assumptions a reasonable man would make in that situation, and did you act in a manner that seems reasonable based on that evidence? This is where the jury comes in, because the jury is a group of (hopefully) reasonable people who are going to look at your actions and your situation and make a call. Basically, do your actions make sense to them? Would they believe similar things in the same situation?

To be legally justified in using lethal force against fellow human beings, you need to meet the following criteria.

They have the "ability" to cause you serious bodily harm.

They have the "opportunity" to cause you serious bodily harm.

They are acting in a manner that suggests they are an "immediate threat" of serious bodily harm.

If your encounter fits these three criteria, then you are usually legally justified in using lethal force.

"Ability" simply means that the person has the power to hurt you. A gun or a knife can obviously cause serious bodily harm. However, a person does not need a weapon to seriously hurt you. Any blow to the head sufficient to render you unconscious or cause internal bleeding is sufficient to kill you.

"Opportunity" means that he can reach you with his ability. A hundred yards away with a gun, he can still hit you, so he has the opportunity. A hundred yards away with a knife, pipe, or chain, and he isn't a danger to you in that instant. However, thirty feet away with a contact weapon is easily within range to cause most people serious bodily harm before they are capable of using a firearm to neutralize the threat. I'll talk more about distances later.

"Immediacy" (often called "jeopardy") means that the person is acting in a manner that suggests he intends to cause serious bodily harm right now. Somebody can have the ability and opportunity, but if a reasonable person wouldn't believe that he is acting like a threat, then he isn't one.

Now let's break this down in more depth.

Under "ability" you will often see self-defense experts refer to "disparity of force." This is where there is such a physical disparity between two individuals that "ability" is assumed. I'm six feet, five inches, I weigh about three hundred pounds, and I've rendered people unconscious with my bare hands. If I'm unarmed but I am attacking an average-sized person and he or she shoots me, then a reasonable person should assume that there was a disparity of force, and the person was justified in shooting me. Usually when a man attacks a woman, or a strong, fit young person attacks a frail old person, then disparity of force is assumed.

However, a person doesn't have to be bigger or stronger to have ability. That merely helps convince the reasonable people you were justified. Regardless of size, if you knock someone down and are sitting on them and raining blows on their head, then you are demonstrating the ability to cause them serious bodily harm. A small woman could brain a big, strong man over the head with a rock and proceed to beat him, thus demonstrating ability.

A person doesn't even need to demonstrate that he's got the ability, he just needs to act in a manner that would suggest to a reasonable person that he does. If you tell somebody, "Give me your purse or I'll shoot you," but you don't show them your gun, a reasonable person would assume that you wouldn't make that threat if you didn't have the ability. He doesn't need to wait to see the muzzle flash to confirm the gun is real. That's suicidal.

You might be very surprised at the relatively lengthy distance an attacker can be from you yet still be a threat with just a contact weapon. It is easy to underestimate how much space a human being can cover in a very short period of time. In many of my CCW classes, I used a series of role-playing scenarios to demonstrate various issues and test the "shoot/no shoot" decision-making process. While playing an aggressor, I routinely covered in excess of twenty feet and caused serious bodily harm before most students could even draw their gun, let alone aim.

Gun people have all heard of the Tueller Drill, which demonstrated that the average person could cover about twenty-one feet before the average police officer could react, draw, and fire a shot (and as we'll see later, one shot doesn't often mean much, even assuming it hits something vital).[1] There are a lot of misconceptions about this drill, but basically, without going into a whole lot of detail, reasonable people are usually stunned to see just how much distance can be covered to provide opportunity.

The last, "immediacy" or "jeopardy," is the most complicated. Say a man with a gun has ability and opportunity, but if he is just minding his own business standing there with the gun in the holster, slung, or being carried in a nonthreatening manner, then he's not presenting a threat. If he is acting like he is going to use it on you, now he is acting like an immediate threat. Again, it all comes down to context and how a reasonable person would perceive it.

This is why it is silly when anti-gun people start ranting about how they're justified in harming people who are openly carrying firearms on their person. Nope. Unless they're acting in a manner that suggests they're an immediate threat, then they're fine. Otherwise it would be legally justifiable to shoot everybody like me that shops at the Big & Tall Outlet because of disparity of force. A person can't just have ability or opportunity, he must be acting in a manner that a reasonable person would take to be a threat. You've got to have all three.

In most states these rules apply to yourself or a third person being the potential recipient of serious bodily harm, however I believe there might be some states where it is only for you, and not a bystander. Some states suck.

You'll hear people talking, usually ignorantly, about "castle doctrine" or "duty to retreat." This can get really confusing because those terms may mean entirely different things in different states. Basically, some states expect you to try and flee before exercising lethal force, and they allow the prosecution to question your inability to escape. Some states require you to flee your own home. Most states don't have that. The idea is that your home is your castle, so the presumption is that anyone trying to breach your castle is demonstrating ability and opportunity and presenting an immediate threat.

Not that escaping or avoiding isn't a great idea *if* given the opportunity, but it sucks to have a prosecutor second-guessing your running ability.

Violent encounters are rarely simple. Think of a triangle. There are three aspects to every violent encounter: the legal side (the decisions that keep you out of jail), the tactical side (the decisions that keep you alive), and the moral side (the decisions that let you sleep at night). These don't always all match up neatly.

Say somebody breaks into your house. Before you've even seen them, you can make some assumptions, they came into your house while you are home. They probably wouldn't do that if they didn't have the ability, now they've certainly got the opportunity, and their presence is an immediate threat. That covers the legality—however you still need to identify the target before firing to make sure that it is actually a threat, and not some mistaken identity, your drunk teenager, or the neighbors' autistic kid.

This triangle isn't a legal doctrine, it is just a tool I used as an instructor to illustrate that this stuff is complicated. I can give you advice about how the law works, and I might be able to help you with your tactics, but you've all got different codes and beliefs, so the moral part is entirely up to you. There are times when morally you want to get involved, but legally you shouldn't. Or you want to help someone, but getting involved might get you killed. There are a multitude of possible situations. There's not always an easy answer to give, and the "right" thing to do depends on your skills, training, knowledge, and commitment. Sometimes the best answer is to run away and dial 911. Other times it might be, *This guy is in need of shooting right now or people are going to die, so let's get to it.*

I worked primarily with regular folks and a little with the police. The law enforcement triangle is different. The situations they are expected to get involved with differ from ours. In fact, in most scenarios for us, avoidance is the best answer, and in the vast majority of real-life violent encounters involving a regular citizen, no shots are fired, because simply producing the gun is enough to deter the attacker. One thing permit holders need to get through their heads is that we aren't cops. The permit is simply a license to carry a concealed firearm in order to defend ourselves from violence. It's not a badge.

Cops on the other hand are expected to respond to violent people and apprehend them. As a result police have what is usually known as the "use of force pyramid." That means that they are supposed to respond with the lowest amount of force necessary to stop any given situation. That is why they are expected to use Tasers or pepper spray before they use physical force or bullets. Their goal is to stop the situation, and they'll try to respond with one level more force than the person they're trying to stop. However, and this is a big damned *however*, just like the rules for regular people above, if they are in immediate danger of serious bodily harm, then they are justified in using lethal force.

Tasers and pepper spray are not magic. Most people's understanding of these tools comes from TV, and TV isn't reality. Tasers don't knock you unconscious. They stream electricity through your body, which causes your muscles to lock up for a moment, and if the circuit ends—for example, the tiny wires break, or the barbs fall out—then you are back to normal and it is game on. And I'm talking about the real Tasers police use. The little stun guns or "drive tasers" are useless toys. It annoys me when unscrupulous types sell these to the gullible public as legitimate self-defense tools. Getting hit with one feels like being pinched with a red-hot pair of pliers, which sucks, but if you're tough enough, you can play tag with the damned things.

Pepper spray hurts and makes it hard to see and breathe, but you can build up a resistance to it—ask anybody who has worked in a prison—and it can also bounce back on the user. Just like with firearms, you need to understand the limitations of your less lethal equipment too. I'm a big fan of pepper spray and usually have a can of POM clipped to my pocket. It's a great intermediate tool that is supplemental to firearms, but it is not a replacement.

In reality different self-defense tools work sometimes, and other times they don't. You'll note that in most videos when you see cops dealing with actual violent types and they are using less lethal tools, there is usually cop number two standing there with a real gun in case plan A doesn't work.

Also cops have hands-on methods available. "Pain compliance techniques" means things like arm bars, wrist locks, and wrestling until you say, "Enough of this crap!" and let them put the cuffs on. However, like anything in life that requires physical force applied by one human being against another, these things are dangerous, and bad things might happen. Bones break, arteries are cut off, people get hurt, and sometimes they die.

The police are going to try to respond to their subject a level above what the subject is using, until he surrenders or complies. Which means that if they think you are going to lethal force, they are going to go to lethal force, and the time it takes to switch gears is measured in fractions of a second.

If you try to wrestle away a cop's gun, that demonstrates ability, opportunity, and immediacy, because right after you get ahold of that firearm the reasonable assumption is going to be that you're intending to use it. If you fight a cop, and he thinks you're going to use lethal force, he's going to repeatedly place bullets into you until you quit.

Everybody who carries a gun, whether law enforcement or not, usually trains to shoot at the upper chest as the primary target and hit that repeatedly until the threat stops. The upper chest, often colloquially referred to as "center of mass" even though COM isn't really biologically accurate, is the primary target because it's big and filled with vital things that will cause a rapid drop in blood pressure when they get punctured. If that doesn't work, the target is the head. If neither of those are available, you shoot whatever part is available.

Contrary to the movies, pistols aren't death rays. A pistol bullet simply pokes a hole. Usually when somebody is stopped by being shot it is (a) psychological, as in "Holy crap! I'm shot! That hurt! I surrender!" or (b) physiological, as in a drop in blood pressure sufficient for the person to cease hostilities. If that hole poked is in a vital organ, then the attacker will stop faster. If it isn't in a vital organ, he will stop slower. Pistols do not pick people up, nor do they throw people back. Pistol bullets are usually insufficiently powerful to break significant bones.

Shooting someone who is actively trying to harm you while under pressure is actually very hard, which is why people often miss. This is why you aim for the biggest available target and continue shooting until the person stops doing whatever it is that caused you to shoot him in the first place.

You'll often hear ignorant people say, "Why didn't they just shoot him in the arm/leg?" That is foolishness. Legally and tactically, shooting someone in the arm or leg is still a use of lethal force. If the assailant bleeds to death in a minute because you severed his femoral artery, he's not any less dead. The difference is he still had one more minute to continue trying to murder you. Basically, limb hits are difficult to pull off with the added bonus of being terribly unreliable stoppers.

What's worse is when they give you the "Why didn't they just shoot the knife/gun out of his hand?" critique. The odds of pulling that off are infinitesimally small. Legally, you are still exercising lethal force, and in the time you are wasting trying to make that nearly impossible shot on a tiny moving target, the bad guy is still doing whatever it was that made it legally justifiable to shoot him in the first place…like killing you or somebody else. It just doesn't work like that in real life, but as we saw in the Do-Somethings, true believers don't let pesky things like reality hold them back.

One great resource to see some of the many ways that violent encounters can unfold is the Active Self Protection channel on You-Tube, where they have collected thousands of videos of real-life events to learn from.[2]

In a fatal shooting, you'll often hear detractors claim, "There was only one side of the story told," as if the winner's perspective is the only one that's going to be heard. That is false. In the after-math of any shooting in a jurisdiction with a functional justice system, whether it is the police or the general public doing the shooting, there is going to be an investigation. There will be evidence gathered. There will be witnesses. There will be an autopsy. There are always multiple sides to the story of a shooting, even if it is just the autopsy results.

Contrary to the media narrative, most police officers don't want to shoot anyone, regardless of the person's skin color. Most regular people who carry guns or keep one at home for defense don't want to shoot anybody either.

One big reason everyone knowledgeable about this sort of thing is reluctant to shoot somebody is because we know that after we have to make that awful "shoot/no shoot" decision in a terrifying fraction of a second, dozens of people are going to spend thousands of man hours gathering evidence, then they are going to argue about our actions, analyze our every move, guess at our thoughts, and debate whether we were reasonable or not, all from the comfort of an air-conditioned room. And when they get hungry, they'll order pizza. When all is said and done, these people will have a million times longer than we did to decide if what we did in those seconds was justified.

No pressure.

Each state is different, but if there is any question as to the justification of the shooting, there is usually some form of grand jury, and if there is sufficient question or evidence of wrongdoing, then the shooter will be indicted.

Now, an argument can be made as to how shootings—especially those committed by law enforcement officers who are expected to exercise a higher standard of care—should be investigated. However, no matter how the shooter is judged, it should be done through our constitutional protections and our agreed upon legal system. No one should ever be convicted through the court of public opinion or the media. *Never* trust the news. Over twenty years of studying violent encounters and learning everything I could about various shootings, I never once found a single newspaper article or report that got all the facts right. Usually they weren't even close. While I was an instructor, I offered free training in use of force to reporters or detractors, and I never once had any of them take me up on it. We even had a really neat simulator that projected video on the wall, and you were armed with a laser gun that tracked and recorded all your hits, and you could go through various scenarios that branched based upon your decisions—yet reporters still couldn't be bothered. Why see how difficult some of these decisions really are, when you can just make ignorant assumptions and print those instead?

Terrible reporting aside, you may believe that grand juries are too soft on police involved shootings. That may be a valid argument. You may believe that prosecutors are too lenient on police officers because they both work for the government and there is an existing relationship between the prosecutors and the police. That may be a valid argument. Burning down Walgreens isn't the answer.

There are stupid cops, and there are cops who make mistakes. As representatives of an extremely powerful state, they should be held to a higher standard. Just because people work for the government doesn't make them infallible, and if they screw up and kill somebody for a stupid reason, they should be punished.

Another huge difference between law enforcement and regular people is that we don't get qualified immunity. Armed citizens don't get to claim that our actions are justified because it happened while we were in the line of duty. If one of us screws up in a lethal force situation, there is no presumption that we meant well. The state will crush you.

Regular citizens don't enjoy the protections of that powerful state, and sometimes they even get steamrolled by it. All it takes is a politically motivated prosecutor, and even the clearest, most straightforward self-defense cases can be twisted into a legal nightmare. Add a compliant media, and even if you get off, they'll still try to ruin your life in the process.

Violent encounters are complex, and the only thing they have in common is that they all suck. Going into any investigation with preconceived notions is foolish. Making decisions as to right or wrong before you've seen any of the evidence is asinine. If you are a nationally elected official, like say, for example, the President of the United States, who repeatedly feels the need to chime in on local crime issues before you know any facts, you are partly to blame for the resulting unrest, and should probably shut up and go hold a beer summit.

■   ■   ■

Once you have a fundamental understanding of how use of force laws are supposed to work, it is harder to be manipulated by the press. Take whatever shooting they are spun up about this week, try to find out the actual cold-hearted facts, and then ask if a reasonable person would believe there was ability, opportunity, and an immediate threat of serious bodily harm. Usually the answer is pretty obvious, and the jury's decision matches that.

This was one reason the American gun culture was glued to the Rittenhouse trial. Would the basic principles of self-defense win out over trial by media and threats of mob violence? The regular news coverage of this one was so biased and horrid that I believe more people followed Rekieta Law's livestream of the trial than corporate media giant CNN. All of the media obfuscation aside, the actual shooting wasn't questionable at all. Rittenhouse was *clearly* in danger of serious bodily harm, from assailants who had the ability, opportunity, and who were *clearly* acting like immediate threats. Which was why the media hype focused on irrelevant minutia like why he was there, or why he was armed (duh)—and that's not even getting into all the blatant lies, or the insipid white knighting for criminals, one of whom had a truly despicable record.

Remember that triangle I talked about? Placing yourself near an angry mob of arsonists and disgruntled nuts is tactically foolish, but it isn't illegal; and in this case Rittenhouse decided being there was the moral thing to do. That was his decision to make, and it also wasn't illegal. I saw lots of people who wanted Rittenhouse convicted because they disagreed with his decisions, but very few of them tried to articulate how any of those decisions was actually against the law.

The Trayvon Martin shooting is another example of how this works. You can disagree with Zimmerman's tactics of putting himself in that situation, or his questionable moral decision to unnecessarily interact with Martin at all, but the actual legal part, getting knocked down and beaten, satisfies the ability, opportunity, and immediate threat aspects. There was a lot of outrage when Zimmerman was acquitted, but none of the people who understand self-defense law were surprised.

More recently the Ahmaud Arbery shooting resulted in three men going to prison, because the jury rejected their claims that it was justified self-defense. They might have thought confronting someone they assumed was a burglar to be the moral thing to do, but it was tactically stupid, and legally questionable. They tried to pursue and detain Arbery at gunpoint, which created a bad situation that led directly to their shooting him. Which the reasonable people of the jury said wasn't justified since the three men were the ones who introduced the opportunity and immediate threat into the situation.

Remember, as a rule of thumb, don't trust anything you hear about a shooting for the first twenty-four to seventy-two hours. During that time period, much of the information is often incorrect, or outright fabrications. This is especially true if the case is politically charged and the media can get some mileage out of it.

This is how you get the stories about the poor innocent teenage girl who was ruthlessly gunned down by bloodthirsty, racist police in Columbus. The news was positively giddy over the possibility of more riots...until the badge camera footage came out and it turned out that the media left out the part where she had a knife and was actively trying to gut another girl like a fish.[3] Then the pundits just switched gears and said that teenage knife fights are just a normal part of growing up and asked why the police officer didn't just shoot the knife out of her hand.

Conclusion

Self-Defense Is a Human Right

It doesn't matter who you are, there is somebody out there who would be happy to kill you. It doesn't matter what your lifestyle choices are, there are evil people who want you to die for them. There are ideologically inspired killers so motivated that they'll weaponize pressure cookers, or regularly carry out gun massacres in countries where it's impossible for regular people to legally own guns. Then there are killers who will flip your off switch just because you looked at them wrong. There are men so violent they will rape, rob, or brutalize others just because they're bored.

This might seem incomprehensible to some, but murderers are not like you.

"Your understanding and consent are not required for someone to take your life, kill your loved ones, and destroy all you hold dear."—Dr. William Aprill[1]

Thinking about this sort of thing makes some people uncomfortable, because if they dwell on it, and ask themselves what they would do in a hypothetical horrible situation, and their only options are run, hide, or call 911, they'll realize they're mostly helpless; and helpless-ness is a deeply troubling thing to come to terms with.

So rather than think about those awful possibilities, they'll just shirk their responsibility and abdicate their personal safety to the gov-ernment. If violence comes for them, it's not their problem. Surely the state will save the day. They don't like to be pushed on this because deep down they know the truth, which is why they become so incred-ibly defensive about the issue. If you choose to be armed, they'll say you're paranoid. If you train and improve your skills, they'll accuse you of living out a sick fantasy. You must *want* to shoot someone. They'll try to twist it so that their self-inflicted helplessness makes them morally superior to those who would fight back to defend themselves.

It's the "perhaps if we're nice they'll go away" defense, except hope is not a strategy, and reality has a tendency to punch you in the face.

And a lot of Americans have gotten metaphorically punched in the face over the last few years. There are endless examples of the state failing to intervene in time, or at all. We keep breaking gun sales records, and those aren't all being sold to the same old gun nuts. An overwhelming number of these purchases have been first timers, many of whom belong to various demographics that have long been counted on to be reliably anti-gun by the institutions waging our relentless culture war.

Part of that culture war has been portraying gun rights as something beloved by old white men, who are probably racist somehow and just itching for a chance to shoot somebody for no reason. We've all had those caricatures shoved down our throats. We all know it's a total crock, but it's the narrative that's been peddled for the longest time.

How many times have you seen a meme on social media with some variation of *I bet the NRA would be in favor of reasonable gun restrictions if large numbers of black men start getting CCWs!* Too bad the NRA was founded by former Union officers because they were unsatisfied with the marksmanship of their soldiers in the war to end slavery, while early gun control was designed to keep freed slaves disarmed and unable to defend themselves against racist Democrats.[2] It is a dirty little secret that American gun control laws originated to keep blacks, immigrants, and other "undesirables" from being armed.

Or one of my personal favorites, how often do you see a meme with a picture of a white family posing with their guns, next to a picture of a black family posing with their guns, and some self-righteous caption that essentially says, *If you're okay with one picture, why do you hate the other?*

Which is some laughable projection, because they're basically the same picture to me. Of the dozens of times I've seen this sort of stupid thing circulate on the internet on my feeds, which are overwhelmingly populated by gun people, hardly anyone cares about the respective races. The harshest comments I usually see are from someone complaining about how one of the kids is holding his gun wrong. My people are downright militant when it comes to keeping your finger out of the trigger guard until you are ready to fire.

These racial comparison memes exist because of projection. The anti-gun zealots are terrified of the idea of minority groups being armed because of their own innate racism (just like the entire history of gun control), so of course they assume their opponents are the same way. But more importantly, the reason the vultures get so upset is that once people have chosen to arm themselves, they are less likely to vote for politicians who are going to disarm them.

Meanwhile my people are downright gleeful. Welcome to the fight, newbs.

This does not mean the gun culture is not without blemish or free from sin. Take any group that represents a giant swath of the country and there's going to be every possible type of jerk, malcontent, and doofus represented in that sample.

Yes, there have been times when gun owners have been insular, elitist, and standoffish or acted like a bunch of high school mean girls declaring who was (or wasn't) allowed to sit at the cool kids table, as they chased everybody who wasn't exactly like them away from gun ownership. However that has changed a lot over the last few decades, as old crusty bastards died off and were replaced by people whose only concern was, *Are you cool and not going to try and strip my rights away? Sweet. Let's go shooting.*

You can still find the occasional bigot, but they're thankfully much rarer now. Bigotry usually manifests as one of those grumpy types who would just be a dick to everyone anyway, and bigotry is just a convenient way to be a dick. Don't worry, the rest of us are annoyed by that guy too.

To give you an idea of how times have changed, when anti-gun zealots try to prove that gun owners would be terrified of armed minority groups enough to do an about-face and suddenly support gun control, they bring up the example of California governor Ronald Reagan passing laws to specifically disarm the Black Panthers. That is true. That did happen.[3] It was also in 1967...eight years before I was born, and I'm not exactly young. Not to mention that if you bring up those laws to the modern gun culture, they're met with sneering disdain. Especially since that was California's first stupid gun control law, and look how that awful cancer has spread ever since.

Compare that to the modern gun culture's nonreaction to the NFAC. During the chaotic summer of 2020, there were a whole bunch of news reports about a black militia group called the *Not Fucking Around Coalition*. Which, for the record, I think is a hilariously awesome name. You've probably all seen the photos of NFAC marching, dressed all in black, wearing vests or plate carriers, and carrying rifles.

Especially the icky, scary "assault rifles" the media hates so much. The news constantly bombarded us with pictures and videos, and I don't know how many times I saw snide yet hopeful comments on social media about how now the white folks would be scared enough to support gun control.

What a bunch of projection that turned out to be, because those on the anti-gun side are the ones who are terrified of people being armed. The gun culture yawned.

The only time I saw NFAC come up in gun circles was when someone would make fun of their leader's videos where he'd hold up his personal weapons while describing them poorly and getting literally every gun fact wrong.[4] Those were comedy gold. There was some atrocious gun handling shown in the news videos of their marches— which caused me to pontificate on the need for quality training—and sure enough one of them had a negligent discharge in Louisville that injured a few people (it wouldn't shock me if the vultures counted that as a "mass shooting").[5] After that they just kind of dropped off the news.

An armed black militia didn't move the needle on the gun control debate at all, simply because most of us are not the racists the media imagines us to be. Oh look, a bunch of people are armed. *Good for them.*

Ironically those same summer months were when a big chunk of America realized they couldn't count on the state to protect them, and we saw the highest number of NICS checks ever to that point, as hordes of people rushed to gun stores seeking tools to defend themselves. New gun purchases jumped a massive 60 percent from the previous year. The National Shooting Sports Foundation estimated 40 percent of those were to first-time purchasers, which came out to a whopping 8.4 million new gun owners. And contrary to the media's fevered imagination about what modern gun owners look like, women made up 40 percent of all gun sales, and purchases by African Americans increased by 56 percent from the year before.[6]

Even as pandemic fears subsided, the trend of increasing minority firearm ownership has continued. Black Americans have outpaced every other demographic, but Hispanic gun ownership increased 49.4 percent and Asian by 42.9 percent.[7]

It isn't just the people buying guns who are rendering the tired old caricatures meaningless, but it is also the people carrying them. Women and minorities have been the primary driver in the number of issued concealed weapons permits, increasing at a faster rate than for white or male.[8] My guess is that as more shall issue states adopt constitutional carry, and the may issue states are slapped down by the Supreme Court and adopt some form of shall issue, this trend will continue.

Recently the *Philadelphia Inquirer* reported that *justifiable* homicides jumped dramatically because of the increase in the number of people legally carrying concealed weapons there, a 67 percent increase between 2020 and 2021, with 2022 on track to be even higher. Even though this news caused a freak-out from the usual suspects, justifiable homicides aren't a bad thing. These were shootings where somebody needed to get shot, and they were demonstrating that ability, opportunity, and immediate threat of serious bodily harm to make their shooting legally justified. This is regular people shooting bad actors.[9]

Why are so many more criminals getting shot by the people who would normally be their helpless victims? Well, the previous high number of permit applications in Philly in recent years was 11,814. In 2021 it was 70,790![10]

Remember when we talked about those big city crime maps, where most of America's murders come from a relative handful of neighborhoods? Those have traditionally been the places where the local residents have been the most hamstrung by idiotic gun control laws. Sadly, because of gun control's racist history, those are almost always minority neighborhoods. Gun control laws didn't do jack to stop the violent criminals terrorizing them, but they kept their victims conveniently disarmed.

Then look at how the gun culture reacted in the aftermath of the Pulse shooting in 2016. A homicidal maniac attacked a gay night club in Florida. Traditionally the gay community has trended overwhelmingly liberal in their politics, with a correspondingly low number of gun owners and CCW. But being unarmed also makes them easier victims for evil people. That had to change.

Operation Blazing Sword was started as a program to get members of the LGBT community armed and proficient by uniting them with firearms instructors who wanted to volunteer their time to teach. I was one of the people who helped them get started because I knew a lot of instructors, so I spread the word to my contacts. They were excited to help, and they gathered their friends and coworkers. Within *days* Operation Blazing Sword had filled a map of the United States with experienced volunteers who were willing to help LGBT people get up to speed, in every state, across the entire nation.

By 2018 the Pink Pistols, an international organization "dedicated to the legal, safe, and responsible use of firearms for self-defense" was incorporated into Operation Blazing Sword, and they are still providing education and activism.[11] A whole bunch of straight, plain-vanilla firearms instructors were happy to help, because regardless of whatever other differences we might have, we all hold the right to self-defense in common.

This isn't your grandpappy's gun culture.

To the people who have been on the fence, or who have been anti-gun because you've been lied to by vultures your whole life, I don't care what your personal beliefs are, or what your lifestyle is, self-defense is a human right. Take advantage of it. Please. If you are responsible and you've got the proper mindset, seek out training, get familiarized with weapons, and then get yourself a firearm. If you live someplace it's possible, get a concealed weapons permit, and get used to carrying it everywhere you can. There are plenty of people happy to walk you through the process.

Full disclosure, my people have selfish reasons for all this proselytizing. It's not entirely altruistic. The more responsible, trained individuals carrying firearms in public, the faster evil people will be met with that immediate violent response, and our families are out there too. Also, as an added bonus, the more people know about guns, the less likely they are to vote for stupid garbage laws that will strip away our rights.

The Second Amendment Is the Only Common Sense Gun Control

As I write this conclusion, Congress is debating another assault weapons ban. As usual everything they're saying is shockingly ignorant or profoundly dishonest. Every dumb Do-Something we talked about before has popped back up. It's downright pathetic. Their proposals are directly contradicted by a Supreme Court decision so recent that the ink hasn't even dried yet. Their entire narrative has been shattered by current events demonstrating criminals don't care about laws, the police won't always come and save you, and good guys with guns are real.

But the vultures will never stop. They can't help themselves. Because gun control isn't about guns. It's about control.

The real question our country faces is this: Does the government own the people, or do the people own their government?

When a government owns its people, then the people are merely assets or liabilities on a balance sheet. Managers eliminate liabilities. The worst atrocities in history have been committed by governments against their own people. Tens of millions dead. Purposefully starved, poisoned in gas chambers, or lined up in front of a ditch and shot in the back of the head. So many corpses they need bulldozers to push them into piles. Murder on an industrial scale.

Their own governments disarmed them first.

This has happened many times before, and it will happen again. When the government owns its people, there is tyranny, and when the people own their government, there is liberty.

That's why we have to win this fight.

The vultures talk about "common sense gun control" as they push nefarious crap, constantly nibbling away at your rights, taking a bit more every time. All of it, every single bite, is designed to make you weaker and them stronger. They push and push and push. The details don't matter. We've clearly seen that they don't even *sort of* understand the laws they write. It's just another infringement to throw on the pile.

Every infringement gets them closer to their goal of making the people entirely dependent upon them. When they are in total control of every aspect of our lives, then we can't resist them. It'll be comply or perish.

Don't make the mistake of thinking the vultures are stupid. Some of them are, but others are cunning. Patient. They watch what works, and what fails, and then they'll hit us again from a different direction. They're relentless true believers. If the usual stupid Do-Somethings can't gain traction to disarm us, they'll destroy with frivolous lawsuits the industry that supplies us or try to pressure banks and credit card companies to stop processing that industry's transactions.

If they can't do it to our industries, they'll do it to us. They've tried to stamp our culture out of existence. Just wait until the government freezes your bank accounts for stating unauthorized opinions. That's happening in other Western nations right now.

Any government powerful enough to give everything is powerful enough to take it all away. Worse, any system that vast and potent will always attract the meanest bullies in society. Even if a government with a totally disarmed and dependent populace hasn't turned into rule by tyrants yet, it will. It isn't *likely* that a system that controlling will become tyrannical, it is *inevitable*.

And our founding fathers knew this.

An armed populace is common sense. Every single one of you being able to defend your lives and liberty is common sense. Protecting your loved ones is common sense. The people being able to stand against any who would enslave them is common sense.

We are fighting for freedom in a world where freedom is becoming scarcer than gold.

The vultures are slimy bastards, but the people they dupe aren't. They're victims of professional con artists, and they don't realize that if the vultures get their way and get that disarmed populace and all-powerful state they've always dreamed of, those dupes will end up in the ditch just like the rest of us. It's why communist revolutions always eventually execute or imprison the academics and activists who originally supported it. Once it is decided that the people are just assets of the state, managers eliminate troublesome assets.

If we're going to win, we need to reach as many of those people as possible. Somebody has to fight the liars and stand up for wisdom and truth.

Just like when evil men attack and violence invades your world, if you're not going to stop it, who else is? If you're already carrying a gun, that means you've thought about that and decided to take responsibility. You're doing your part to stop it. The culture war isn't any different. If you're not going to fight it, then who is?

There are all sorts of different ways to fight for the Second Amendment. It's not all butting heads with jerks and heated arguments on the internet. It's not all donating money or calling politicians and telling them that if they vote for this latest nonsense, you're going to make it your mission in life to kick them out of office. Though all that stuff helps, it's the little things. It's being that good example. That helping hand. It's teaching and passing on knowledge.

The greatest warrior for the Second Amendment is the grandpa who takes the grandkids out and shows them how to knock cans off a fence with a pellet gun.

It's the patient spouse who tries to gently persuade his or her significant other that Moms Demand Action is lying to them, and that allowing a gun in their home isn't the end of the world.

It's the manager who tells the HR department to shut up, and then tears down all those gun-free zone signs.

It's *you* every time you take some new people to the range, show them how to use your guns safely, and then help them have fun.

Gun culture, this is on us. The future of our country depends on us holding the line.

But you've got this because you're awesome. I've got faith in you.

Notes

Chapter One

1. David Shortell, "Congressional Baseball Shooter Fired at Least 70 Rounds, Cased Area for Months," CNN, October 6, 2017, https://www.cnn.com /2017/10/06/politics/congressional-shooter-70-rounds/index.html; Matt Keeley, "Rep. Steve Scalise, Shot by Sanders Supporter, Replies to Request for Evidence of 'Bernie Bros' Being Bad: 'I Can Think of an Example,'" *Newsweek*, February 20, 2020, https://www.newsweek.com/rep-steve -scalise-shot-sanders-supporter-replies-request-evidence-bernie-bros-being -bad-1488354; Wikipedia, "2016 Shooting of Dallas Police Officers," September 17, 2022, https://en.wikipedia.org/wiki/2016_shooting_of _Dallas_police_officers; Joseph Choi, "McConnell: Black Lives Matter Bailing Out Shooting Suspect in Kentucky 'Jaw-Dropping,'" *The Hill*, February 17, 2022, https://thehill.com/homenews/state-watch/594750 -suspect-in-mayoral-shooting-attempt-released-after-local-group-posts/.
2. Sara Sidner and Mallory Simon, "How Robot, Explosives Took Out Dallas Sniper in Unprecedented Way," CNN, July 12, 2016, https://www.cnn.com /2016/07/12/us/dallas-police-robot-c4-explosives.
3. David Leavitt (@David_Leavitt), "348 Mass Shootings in half a year is 348 too many mass shootings….," Twitter, July 17, 2022, 1:03 a.m., https:// twitter.com/David_Leavitt/status/1548896168402460676; see also Júlia Ledur, Kate Rabinowitz, and Artur Galocha, "There Have Been over 300 Mass Shootings So Far in 2022, *Washington Post*, July 5, 2022, https://www .washingtonpost.com/nation/2022/06/02/mass-shootings-in-2022/.
4. "Mass Shootings in 2022," Gun Violence Archive, 2022, https://www .gunviolencearchive.org/query/0484b316-f676-44bc-97ed-ecefeabae077/map.
5. "FBI Will Investigate San Bernadino Shootings as Terrorist Act," FBI, December 4, 2015, https://www.fbi.gov/news/stories/fbi-will-investigate -san-bernardino-shootings-as-terrorist-act.
6. John R. Lott Jr., "There Are Far More Defensive Gun Uses than Murders. Here's Why You Rarely Hear of Them," RealClear Investigations, September 22, 2021, https://www.realclearinvestigations.com/articles/2021/09/22/there _are_far_more_defensive_gun_uses_than_murders_in_america_heres_why _you_rarely_hear_of_them_794461.html.
7. Ibid.
8. "Statement by President Biden on the Killing of Former Japanese Prime Minister Abe Shinzo," The White House, July 8, 2022, https://www .whitehouse.gov/briefing-room/statements-releases/2022/07/08/statement -by-president-biden-on-the-killing-of-former-japanese-prime-minister-abe -shinzo/.

9. MSNBC, "Biden Comments on Assassination of Former Japanese PM Shinzo Abe," YouTube, July 8, 2022, https://www.youtube.com/watch?v= ELlXZkvYEZc. Though 2022 numbers are incomplete, a review of the available homicide data from 2022 and previous years in Japan and the U.S. clearly contradicts Biden's claims. See Nick Arama, "Biden Descends into Delusion When He Talks about His Gun Control Narrative and Shinzo Abe," RedState, July 8, 2022, https://redstate.com/nick-arama/2022/07/08/biden -descends-into-delusion-when-he-talks-about-his-gun-control-narrative-and -shinzo-abe-n591268; Mai Sato, "Despite Japan's Low Crime Rates, It's Seen a Number of Mass Stabbings in the Past Decade," The Conversation, May 29, 2019, https://theconversation.com/despite-japans-low-crime-rates-its-seen -a-number-of-mass-stabbings-in-the-past-decade-117910; "Number of Homicide Cases Recorded by the Police in Japan from 2012 to 2021," statista, 2022, https://www.statista.com/statistics/1039166/japan-number-of-murders/; "Stabbing Deaths by Country 2022," World Population Review, 2022, https:// worldpopulationreview.com/country-rankings/stabbing-deaths-by-country; "Assault or Homicide," CDC, September 6, 2022, https://www.cdc.gov/nchs /fastats/homicide.htm; Josiah Bates, "U.S. Crime Is Still Dramatically Higher Than before the Pandemic," *Time*, July 29, 2022, https://time.com/6201797 /crime-murder-rate-us-high-2022/; Stephanie Pagones, "US Murder Rate Highest It's Been in 25 Years as Big Cities Shatter Records," Fox News, January 18, 2022, https://www.foxnews.com/us/us-murder-rate-violence-big-cities -records; "Murder Victims by Weapon, 2015–2019," FBI, 2019, https://ucr .fbi.gov/crime-in-the-u.s/2019/crime-in-the-u.s.-2019/tables/expanded -homicide-data-table-8.xls.

10. Kallie Szczepanski, "What Was the Sword Hunt in Japan?," ThoughtCo., July 18, 2018, https://www.thoughtco.com/what-was-the-sword-hunt-in -japan-195284.

11. Michael Lee, "Indiana Police Say 'Good Samaritan' Took Out Mall Shooter in 15 Seconds, Landed 8 of 10 Shots," Fox News, July 20, 2022, https:// www.foxnews.com/us/indiana-police-say-good-samaritan-took-out-mall -shooter-15-seconds-landed-8-of-10-shots.

12. Bad Legal Takes (@BadLegalTakes), "No. He was an 'armed citizen'...," Twitter, July 18, 2022, 2:18 p.m., https://twitter.com/BadLegalTakes/status /1549096197788291072/photo/1; Bad Legal Takes (@BadLegalTakes), "Both the assailant and that 'brave armed citizen'...," Twitter, July 18, 2022, 5:39 p.m., https://twitter.com/BadLegalTakes/status/1549146960451407873/photo/1.

13. Alexandria Burris, Ryan Martin, and Tony Cook, "An Armed Bystander Shot & Killed the Greenwood Mall Shooting Suspect. Did He Break the Law?," *Indianapolis Star*, July 18, 2022, https://www. indystar.com/story/news/crime/2022/07/18/greenwood-mall-other- simon-malls-have-no-weapons-policy-bystander-carried-legally/653 75923007/.

14. Seth, Esq. (@libertarianJD), "Replying to @MorosKostas," Twitter, July 17, 2022, 11:08 p.m., https://twitter.com/libertarianJD/status/1548867274 412621826/photo/1.

15. Guy Relford (@guyrelford), "MEDIA RELEASE," Twitter, July 19, 2022, 4:21 p.m., https://twitter.com/guyrelford/status/1549489594705526785 /photo/1.
16. Leavitt (@David_Leavitt), "348 Mass Shootings in half a year…"
17. Larry Correia, "A Handy Guide for Liberals Who Are Suddenly Interested in Gun Ownership," Monster Hunter Nation, November 14, 2016, https:// monsterhunternation.com/2016/11/14/a-handy-guide-for-liberals-who-are -suddenly-interested-in-gun-ownership/.
18. Ibid.

Chapter Two

1. Roxanne Roberts, "Is Cowardice a Crime? Scot Peterson's Failure Leaves Us with Complicated Questions," *Washington Post*, June 14, 2019, https:// www.washingtonpost.com/lifestyle/style/is-cowardice-a-crime-scot -petersons-failure-leaves-us-with-complicated-questions/2019/06/14 /5853ba6e-8948-11e9-a870-b9c411dc4312_story.html.
2. Davi Barker, "Auditing Shooting Rampage Statistics," Law Enforcement Services, December 15, 2012, https://web.archive.org/web/20 220328073705/http://www.lawenforcementservices.biz/Law_Enforcement _Services,_LLC/FIREARMS_TRAINING_files/Shooting%20St atistics.pdf.
3. "S.3266—Crime Control Act of 1990," Congress.gov, October 27, 1990, https://www.congress.gov/bill/101st-congress/senate-bill/3266.
4. "School Safety: Guns in Schools," National Conference of State Legislatures, May 30, 2022, https://www.ncsl.org/research/education /school-safety-guns-in-schools.aspx.
5. Alexandra Hutzler, "Armed Teacher Hailed as 'Hero' after Stopping Alleged Attempted Kidnapping of 11-Year-Old Girl," *Newsweek*, May 27, 2021, https://www.newsweek.com/armed-teacher-hailed-hero-after -stopping-alleged-attempted-kidnapping-11-year-old-girl-1595548.

Chapter Three

1. Susanna Lee, "How the 'Good Guy with a Gun' Became a Deadly American Fantasy," PBS, June 8, 2019, https://www.pbs.org/newshour/nation/ how-the-good-guy-with-a-gun-became-a-deadly-american-fantasy.
2. See, for example, Susan Milligan, "Uvalde, Buffalo Shootings Expose the Myth of the 'Good Guy with a Gun,'" *U.S. News & World Report*, May 27, 2022, https://www.usnews.com/news/the-report/articles/2022-05-27/ uvalde-buffalo-shootings-expose-the-myth-of-the-good-guy-with-a-gun.
3. Frank Heinz, "'Good Guy with a Gun' Who Stopped Church Gunman Receives Texas' Highest Honor," 5 NBCDFW, January 14, 2020, https:// www.nbcdfw.com/news/local/man-who-took-out-church-gunman-to -receive-states-highest-civilian-honor/2290236/.
4. Saeed Ahmed, Doug Criss, and Emanuella Grinberg, "'Hero' Exchanged Fire with Gunman, then Helped Chase Him Down," CNN, November 7,

2017, https://www.cnn.com/2017/11/05/us/texas-church-shooting-resident-action/index.html.

5.   "UPDATED: Compiling Cases Where Concealed Handgun Permit Holders Have Stopped Likely Mass Public Shootings," Crime Prevention Research Center, August 24, 2022, https://crimeresearch.org/2022/07/uber-driver-in-chicago-stops-mass-public-shooting/.

6.   Ibid.

7.   "Defensive Gun Use," Crime Prevention Research Center, 2022, https://crimeresearch.org/tag/defensive-gun-use/.

8.   "Number of Reported Murder and Nonnegligent Manslaughter Cases in the United States from 1990 to 2020," statista, July 27, 2022, https://www.statista.com/statistics/191134/reported-murder-and-nonnegligent-manslaughter-cases-in-the-us-since-1990/.

9.   Michael Ray, "Orlando Shooting of 2016," in *Encyclopedia Britannica Online*, August 8, 2016, https://www.britannica.com/event/Orlando-shooting-of-2016.

10.   Christian Spencer, "Police Chief Hails 'Good Guy with a Gun' after Officer Kills Him in Tragic Mistaken Identity," *The Hill*, June 29, 2021, https://thehill.com/changing-america/respect/equality/560798-police-chief-hails-good-guy-with-a-gun-after-officer-kills/.

11.   Washington Post, "Uvalde Parents Were Armed and Ready to Storm the School," YouTube, May 27, 2022, https://www.youtube.com/watch?v=7r-TVEOm75M.

Chapter Four

1.   Searcy v. City of Dayton, 38 F.3d 282 (6th Cir. 1994), https://law.resource.org/pub/us/case/reporter/F3/038/38.F3d.282.93-4092.93-4013.html.

2.   Scott Glover, "ATF on the Hunt for Thousands of Illegal Machine Gun Conversion Devices Smuggled into US," CNN, May 23, 2019, https://www.cnn.com/2019/05/23/us/atf-agents-hunting-down-illegal-machine-gun-device-invs/index.html.

3.   "Twenty-Five States Have Constitutional Carry," Crime Prevention Research Center, April 11, 2022, https://crimeresearch.org/2022/04/twenty-five-states-have-constitutional-carry/; Mark Moore, Zach Williams, Samuel Chamberlain, and Gabrielle Fonrouge, "Supreme Court Overturns New York Law on Carrying Concealed Weapons," *New York Post*, June 23, 2022, https://nypost.com/2022/06/23/supreme-court-overturns-ny-law-on-carrying-concealed-weapons/.

4.   Christopher S. Koper, Daniel J. Woods, and Jeffrey A. Roth, *An Updated Assessment of the Federal Assault Weapons Ban: Impacts on Gun Markets and Gun Violence, 1994–2003* (Philadelphia: Jerry Lee Center of Criminology, June 2004), https://www.ojp.gov/pdffiles1/nij/grants/204431.pdf.

5.   Jeff Cook, "Carolyn McCarthy," YouTube, April 18, 2007, https://www.youtube.com/watch?v=ospNRk2uM3U.

6. "Murder Victims by Weapon, 2015–2019," FBI, 2019, https://ucr.fbi.gov /crime-in-the-u.s/2019/crime-in-the-u.s.-2019/tables/expanded-homicide -data-table-8.xls.

7. David Kopel, "What Arms Are 'Common'?," *Reason*, February 12, 2020, https://reason.com/volokh/2020/02/12/what-arms-are-common/.

8. Nicole Silverio, "'That's the Point': Rep. Nadler Admits Bill Will Confiscate Guns in 'Common Use,'" The Daily Caller, July 20, 2022, https:// dailycaller.com/2022/07/20/jerry-nadler-gun-bill-common-use/.

9. Michal Conger, "More Advice from Joe Biden: 'Just Fire the Shotgun through the Door,'" *Washington Examiner*, February 27, 2013, https:// www.washingtonexaminer.com/more-advice-from-joe-biden-just-fire-the -shotgun-through-the-door.

10. Charles A. Jones, "In 1918, the U.S. Armed Its Forces with Shotguns—and Germany Launched a Diplomatic Protest," HistoryNet, December 3, 2019, https://www.historynet.com/the-1918-shotgun-protest/.

11. NowThis News, "Biden Calls a Hunter a 'Terrible Shot,' Justifies Gun Control #Shorts," YouTube, April 11, 2022, https://www.youtube.com /watch?v=RTbTiJShEdg.

12. Rob Reed, "Maryland's 15 Year Old 'Ballistic Fingerprinting' Database Ends in Failure," AllOutdoor, November 8, 2015, https://www.alloutdoor .com/2015/11/08/marylands-15-year-old-ballistic-fingerprinting-database -ends-in-failure/.

13. Mariel Alper and Lauren Glaze, *Source and Use of Firearms Involved in Crimes: Survey of Prison Inmates, 2016* (Washington, D.C.: Bureau of Justice Statistics, January 2019), https://bjs.ojp.gov/content/pub/pdf /suficspi16.pdf.

14. Tara Palmeri and Ben Schreckinger, "Sources: Secret Service Inserted Itself into Case of Hunter Biden's Gun," *POLITICO*, March 25, 2021, https:// www.politico.com/news/2021/03/25/sources-secret-service-inserted-itself -into-case-of-hunter-bidens-gun-477879.

15. Jerry Seper, "Justice Department Rarely Prosecutes 'Straw Buyers,' ATF Nominee Todd Jones Says," *Washington Times*, June 11, 2013, https:// www.washingtontimes.com/news/2013/jun/11/justice-department-rarely -prosecutes-straw-buyers-/.

16. Travis Pike, "Guns Are Being 3D Printed in Myanmar," *National Interest*, January 14, 2022, https://nationalinterest.org/blog/reboot/guns-are-being -3d-printed-myanmar-199401.

17. "Extreme Risk Protection Orders," Johns Hopkins Bloomberg School of Public Health, 2020, https://www.jhsph.edu/research/centers-and-institutes /johns-hopkins-center-for-gun-violence-prevention-and-policy/research/ extreme-risk-protection-orders/.

18. Sady Swanson, "Fort Collins Woman Found Guilty of Lying on Red Flag Petition against CSU Police Officer," *Coloradoan*, April 22, 2022, https:// www.coloradoan.com/story/news/2022/04/22/fort-collins-woman-who -filed-red-flag-petition-against-officer-convicted/7401449001/.

19. See, e.g., "The Effects of Extreme Risk Protection Orders," RAND
   Corporation, April 22, 2020, https://www.rand.org/research/gun-policy
   /analysis/extreme-risk-protection-orders.html; John R. Lott and Carlisle E.
   Moody, "Do Red Flag Laws Save Lives or Reduce Crime?," SSRN, January
   27, 2019, https://papers.ssrn.com/sol3/papers.cfm?abstract_id=3316573.
20. Robert Chiarito and Mitch Smith, "Highland Park Suspect Was Known
   to Police; Bought Guns Legally," *New York Times*, July 5, 2022, https://
   www.nytimes.com/2022/07/05/us/many-details-about-the-attack-remained
   -unclear-a-day-after-the-shooting.html; Ashley Southall, Chelsia Rose
   Marcius, and Andy Newman, "Before the Massacre, the Gunman's Erratic
   Behavior Attracted Attention," *New York Times*, May 15, 2022, https://
   www.nytimes.com/2022/05/15/nyregion/gunman-buffalo-shooting
   -suspect.html?smid=url-share.

Chapter Five

1. Gary Kleck, *Targeting Guns: Firearms and Their Control* (New York:
   Routledge, 2017), 86.
2. Kenneth Garger, "US Saw Record Increase in Murders in 2020," *New York
   Post*, September 22, 2021, https://nypost.com/2021/09/22/us-saw-record
   -increase-in-murders-in-2020/.
3. "Murder Victims by Weapon, 2015–2019," FBI, 2019, https://ucr.fbi.gov
   /crime-in-the-u.s/2019/crime-in-the-u.s.-2019/tables/expanded-homicide
   -data-table-8.xls.
4. Isabel Vincent, "BLM Spent at Least $12M on Luxury Properties in LA,
   Toronto: Tax Filing," *New York Post*, May 17, 2022, https://nypost.com
   /2022/05/17/black-lives-matter-spent-at-least-12-million-on-mansions/.
5. Alissa Tabirian, "CDC Study: Use of Firearms for Self-Defense Is 'Important
   Crime Deterrent,'" CNSNews, July 17, 2013, https://www.cnsnews.com
   /news/article/cdc-study-use-firearms-self-defense-important-crime
   -deterrent; "Defensive Gun Uses in the U.S.," The Heritage Foundation,
   August 15, 2022, https://datavisualizations.heritage.org/firearms/defensive
   -gun-uses-in-the-us/. But, as I say, nobody has a clue, and they are just
   pulling guesses out of thin air.
6. John R. Lott Jr., "There Are Far More Defensive Gun Uses than Murders.
   Here's Why You Rarely Hear of Them.," RealClear Investigations,
   September 22, 2021, https://www.realclearinvestigations.com/articles/2021
   /09/22/there_are_far_more_defensive_gun_uses_than_murders_in
   _america_heres_why_you_rarely_hear_of_them_794461.html.
7. Dave Kopel, "The Fallacy of '43 to 1,'" Dave Kopel, January 31, 2001,
   https://davekopel.org/NRO/2001/The-Fallacy-of-43-to-1.htm; "Myth
   #2—'Guns Aren't an Effective Defense, or, the 43:1 Myth,'" Buckeye
   Firearms Association, https://www.buckeyefirearms.org/myth-2-guns
   -arent-effective-defense-or-431-myth; Greg Camp, "Kellermann's Gun
   Ownership Studies after Two Decades," Guns.com, August 24, 2015,
   https://www.guns.com/news/2015/08/24/kellermanns-gun-ownership

-studies-after-two-decades. For Kellerman's studies, see Arthur L. Kellermann and D. T. Reay, "Protection or Peril? An Analysis of Firearm-Related Deaths in the Home," *New England Journal of Medicine* 314, no. 24 (1986): 1557–60, https://pubmed.ncbi.nlm.nih.gov/3713749/; Arthur L. Kellermann et al., "Gun Ownership as a Risk Factor for Homicide in the Home," *New England Journal of Medicine* 329, no. 15 (1993): 1084–91, https://www.nejm.org/doi/full/10.1056/NEJM199310073291506#t= abstract.

8. Tim Hsiao, "Guns Used More for Self-Defense than Crimes," *Washington Times*, October 5, 2021, https://www.washingtontimes.com/news/2021/oct /5/guns-used-more-for-self-defense-than-crimes/.

9. Samantha Raphelson, "How Often Do People Use Guns in Self-Defense?," NPR, April 13, 2018, https://www.npr.org/2018/04/13/602143823/how -often-do-people-use-guns-in-self-defense.

10. Compare, for example, data on gun ownership and suicides from the World Population Review: "Gun Ownership by Country 2022," World Population Review, 2022, https://worldpopulationreview.com/country-rankings/gun -ownership-by-country; "Suicide Rate by Country 2022," World Population Review, 2022, https://worldpopulationreview.com/country-rankings/ suicide-rate-by-country.

11. Cf. "Gun Violence by Police," Everytown Research and Policy, 2022, https://everytownresearch.org/issue/gun-violence-by-police/; "Mass Shootings Facts and Fiction," USCCA, 2022, https://www.usconcealedcarry .com/resources/gun-facts-and-fiction/mass-shootings/; Mark Follman, "How Many Mass Shootings Are There, Really?," *New York Times*, December 3, 2015, https://www.nytimes.com/2015/12/04/opinion/how -many-mass-shootings-are-there-really.html; "Number of Mass Shootings in the United States between 1982 and July 2022," statista, 2022, https:// www.statista.com/statistics/811487/number-of-mass-shootings-in-the-us/; Mark Follman, Gavin Aronsen, and Deanna Pan, "A Guide to Mass Shootings in America," *Mother Jones*, July 17, 2022, https://www .motherjones.com/politics/2012/07/mass-shootings-map/; "Mass Shootings in 2022," Gun Violence Archive, October 2, 2022, https://www .gunviolencearchive.org/reports/mass-shooting.

12. Movieclips, "*Magnum Force* (10/10) Movie CLIP—A Man's Got to Know His Limitations (1973) HD," YouTube, February 6, 2014, https://www .youtube.com/watch?v=uki4lrLzRaU.

13. Kori Rumore, "Chicago Homicides in 2022: 519 People Have Been Slain. Here's How That Compares with Previous Years," *Chicago Tribune*, October 3, 2022, https://www.chicagotribune.com/news/breaking/ct -chicago-homicides-data-tracker-20220426-iedehzuq5jdofbhwt3v2w6cjoy -story.html.

14. "Constitutional Carry in 25 States," USCCA, March 23, 2022, https:// www.usconcealedcarry.com/blog/constitutional-carry-in-states/; "State-by-State Concealed Carry Permit Laws," Britannica ProCon.org, April 14,

2022, https://concealedguns.procon.org/state-by-state-concealed-carry
-permit-laws/.

15. "Mumbai Terror Attacks Fast Facts," CNN, December 3, 2021, https://
www.cnn.com/2013/09/18/world/asia/mumbai-terror-attacks/index.html.

16. "Vermont: Concealed Carry Reciprocity Map & Gun Laws," USCCA,
March 28, 2022, https://www.usconcealedcarry.com/resources/ccw
_reciprocity_map/vt-gun-laws/.

17. "The Effects of Firearm Safety Training Requirements," RAND
Coporation, April 22, 2020, https://www.rand.org/research/gun-policy
/analysis/firearm-safety-training-requirements.html.

18. "Violent Crime Rates by Country 2022," World Population Review, 2022,
https://worldpopulationreview.com/country-rankings/violent-crime-rates
-by-country.

19. "Australia Population 2022 (Live)," World Population Review, 2022,
https://worldpopulationreview.com/countries/australia-population; United
States Population 2022 (Live), World Population Review, 2022, https://
worldpopulationreview.com/countries/united-states-population.

20. "Violent Crime Rates by Country 2022"; Australian Institute of Health
and Welfare, *Sexual Assault in Australia* (Canberra: Australian Institute
of Health Welfare, 2020), https://www.aihw.gov.au/reports/domestic
-violence/sexual-assault-in-australia/contents/summary; Sue Dunlevy,
"Australia's Sexual Assault Shame: One in Six Women a Victim, Putting
Australia Way above World Average," news.com.au, February 12, 2014,
https://www.news.com.au/national/australias-sexual-assault-shame-one
-in-six-women-a-victim-putting-australia-way-above-world-average/news
-story/46e88d9ceac5b354f9a8d1d6e055b2dd.

21. E.g., Joyce Lee Malcolm, "Joyce Lee Malcolm: Two Cautionary Tales of
Gun Control," *Wall Street Journal*, December 26, 2012, https://www.wsj
.com/articles/SB10001424127887323777204578195470446855466.

22. "Compare Violent Crime Rates in USA and Britain," www.Discourage
Criminals.net, http://www.discouragecriminals.net/compare-us-with-
british-violent-crime/#britains-significantly-underrecorded-violent-crime-
rate.

23. Tariq Tahir and Sofia Petkar, "COLD KILLER: What Happened on 22
July in Oslo and Utoya during the 2011 Norway Attacks and Where Is
Killer Anders Breivik Now?," *The Sun*, October 18, 2018, https://www
.thesun.co.uk/news/7477508/22-july-oslo-utoya-2011-norway-attacks
-anders-breivik/.

24. Terje Solsvik and Gwladys Fouche, "Horror on Oslo Pride Day as Gunman
Goes on Deadly Rampage at Gay Bar," Reuters, June 25, 2022, https://
www.reuters.com/world/europe/two-dead-several-wounded-norway
-nightclub-shooting-police-say-2022-06-25/.

25. Michael Ray, "Paris Attacks of 2015," in *Encyclopedia Britannica Online*,
June 30, 2022, https://www.britannica.com/event/Paris-attacks-of-2015
/The-response-to-the-Paris-attacks; "2015 Paris Terror Attacks Fast Facts,"

CNN, October 31, 2021, https://www.cnn.com/2015/12/08/europe/2015
-paris-terror-attacks-fast-facts/index.html.

26. Rina Bassist, "Nice Marks 2016 Bastille Day Terrorist Attack," *Jerusalem
    Post*, July 15, 2018, https://www.jpost.com/International/Nice-marks-2016
    -Bastille-Day-terrorist-attack-562496.

27. Crimesider Staff, "25th Anniversary of Happy Land Nightclub Fire That
    Killed 87," CBS News, March 25, 2015, https://www.cbsnews.com/news
    /25th-anniversary-of-happy-land-nightclub-fire-that-killed-87/.

28. Lorraine Boissoneault, "The 1927 Bombing That Remains America's
    Deadliest School Massacre," *Smithsonian Magazine*, May 18, 2017, https://
    www.smithsonianmag.com/history/1927-bombing-remains-americas
    -deadliest-school-massacre-180963355/.

29. Fikayo Owoeye, "At Least 50 Killed in Massacre at Catholic Church in
    Southwest Nigeria," Reuters, June 6, 2022, https://www.reuters.com/world
    /africa/gunmen-kill-worshippers-during-church-service-nigeria-media
    -2022-06-05/.

30. Grant Peck and Busaba Sivasomboon, "Thai Mass Shooting That Killed
    29 Lasted 16 Hours," ABC News, February 9, 2020, https://abcnews.go
    .com/International/wireStory/timeline-mass-shooting-thailand-killed-27
    -68859967; Richard C. Paddock, Ryn Jirenuwat, Muktita Suhartono, "At
    a Temple, Thai Gunman's Revenge Gave Way to a Random Killing
    Rampage," *New York Times*, February 11, 2020, https://www.nytimes
    .com/2020/02/11/world/asia/thai-gunman-temple.html.

31. "Kyoto Animation Fire: Arson Attack at Japan Anime Studio Kills 33,"
    BBC News, July 18, 2019, https://www.bbc.com/news/world-asia
    -49027178.

32. "Japan Knife Attack: 19 Killed at Care Centre in Sagamihara," BBC News,
    July 26, 2016, https://www.bbc.com/news/world-asia-36890655.

33. David Willetts, "WHO DARES WINS: Tooled-Up SAS Hero Led Charge
    into Kenya Hotel to Kill Terrorists and Rush Victims to Safety as Fanatics
    Slaughtered 14," *The Sun*, January 16, 2019, https://www.thesun.co.uk
    /news/8207170/nairobi-hotel-attack-kenya-sas-terrorists/.

34. Daniel Howden, "Terror in Nairobi: The Full Story behind Al-Shabaab's
    Mall Attack," *The Guardian*, October 4, 2013, https://www.theguardian
    .com/world/2013/oct/04/westgate-mall-attacks-kenya; Jeff Knox, "Citizen
    Gun Owners—First Responders in Kenyan Terror Attack," Ammoland,
    October 11, 2013, https://www.ammoland.com/2013/10/citizen-gun
    -owners-first-responders-in-kenyan-terror-attack/.

35. "U.S. Murder/Homicide Rate 1990–2022," macrotrends, 2022, https://
    www.macrotrends.net/countries/USA/united-states/murder-homicide-rate.

36. Elisha Fieldstadt, "Murder Map: Deadliest U.S. Cities," CBS News,
    February 23, 2022, https://www.cbsnews.com/pictures/murder-map
    -deadliest-u-s-cities/40/.

37. "Homicides by Chicago Neighborhood, 2015," The Trace, 2015, https://
    www.thetrace.org/wp-content/uploads/2016/07/Chicago-Heat-Map-copia.jpg.

38. "Firearm Registration Requirements by State," Ballotpedia, https://ballotpedia.org/Firearm_registration_requirements_by_state.
39. Gregory Yee, "Leak of California Concealed-Carry Permit Data Is Larger than Initially Reported," *Los Angeles Times*, June 29, 2022, https://www.latimes.com/california/story/2022-06-29/california-concealed-carry-weapons-permit-data-exposed-in-leak.
40. "Eric Swalwell, a Chinese 'Honeytrap' and FBI Double Standards" (editorial), *New York Post*, December 9, 2020, https://nypost.com/2020/12/09/eric-swalwell-a-chinese-honeytrap-and-fbi-double-standards/; Lia Eustachewich, "Rep. Eric Swalwell Appears to Fart on Live TV," *New York Post*, November 19, 2019, https://nypost.com/2019/11/19/congressman-eric-swalwell-appears-to-fart-on-live-tv/.
41. Awr Hawkins, "Democrat Eric Swalwell: If Gun Owners Defy 'Assault Weapons' Ban, 'The Government Has Nukes,'" Breitbart, November 16, 2018, https://www.breitbart.com/politics/2018/11/16/eric-swalwell-if-gun-owners-defy-assault-weapons-ban-the-government-has-nukes/.
42. Micah Zenko, "Obama's Final Drone Strike Data," Council on Foreign Relations, January 20, 2017, https://www.cfr.org/blog/obamas-final-drone-strike-data.
43. "Estimate of the U.S. Post-9/11 War Spending, in $ Billions FY2001–FY2022," Watson Institute International & Public Affairs, Brown University, September 2021, https://watson.brown.edu/costsofwar/figures/2021/BudgetaryCosts.
44. Michael E. O'Hanlon and Andrew Kamons, *Iraq Index: Tracking Variables of Reconstruction & Security in Post-Saddam Iraq* (Washington, D.C.: Brookings Institution, 2006), https://www.brookings.edu/wp-content/uploads/2017/11/index20060731.pdf.
45. "NICS Firearm Checks: Month/Year," FBI, August 31, 2022, https://www.fbi.gov/file-repository/nics_firearm_checks_-_month_year.pdf/view.
46. Mark Joslyn and Donald P. Haider-Markel, "Americans Vastly Overestimate the Number of Gun Owners," *Washington Post*, May 7, 2018, https://www.washingtonpost.com/news/monkey-cage/wp/2018/05/07/americans-vastly-overestimate-the-number-of-gun-owners-thats-a-problem/.
47. Michael Maciag, "Military Active-Duty Personnel, Civilians by State," Governing, October 2017, https://www.governing.com/archive/military-civilian-active-duty-employee-workforce-numbers-by-state.html.
48. Jesse J. Smith, "Massive Noncompliance with SAFE Act," *Hudson Valley One*, April 1, 2019, https://hudsonvalleyone.com/2016/07/07/massive-noncompliance-with-safe-act/.

Chapter Six

1. Mark Wilson, "How Failures during the Waco Siege Changed Everything for the FBI, ATF," *Austin American-Statesman*, April 19, 2018, https://www.statesman.com/story/news/2018/04/19/how-failures-during-the-waco-siege-changed-everything-for-the-fbi-atf/10039028007/.

2. Carter Williams, "Looking Back at the Trolley Square Shooting 10 Years Later," KSL.com, February 12, 2017, https://www.ksl.com/article/43161303/looking-back-at-the-trolley-square-shooting-10-years-later.

3. Amanda Prestigiacomo, "What Percentage of Mass Shootings Happen in 'Gun Free Zones'? The Number Is Stunning," DailyWire+, February 22, 2018, https://www.dailywire.com/news/what-percentage-mass-shootings-happen-gun-free-amanda-prestigiacomo.

4. For more evidence on the inefficacy of gun-free zones, see "Mass Shootings Facts and Fiction," USCCA, 2019, https://www.usconcealedcarry.com/resources/gun-facts-and-fiction/mass-shootings/; and John R. Lott, "UPDATED: Mass Public Shootings Keep Occurring in Gun-Free Zones: 94% of Attacks since 1950," Crime Prevention Research Center, June 6, 2019, https://crimeresearch.org/2018/06/more-misleading-information-from-bloombergs-everytown-for-gun-safety-on-guns-analysis-of-recent-mass-shootings/. Everytown for Gun Safety's claim is cited in Amy Sherman, "Do Most Mass Shootings Happen in Gun-Free Zones?," PolitiFact, February 21, 2017, https://www.politifact.com/factchecks/2017/feb/21/richard-corcoran/do-most-mass-shootings-happen-gun-free-zones/; see also "Mass Shootings in America," Everytown for Gun Safety, June 4, 2021, https://everytownresearch.org/maps/mass-shootings-in-america/.

5. Jen Kirby, "A Suicide in a School. A Bullet on Campus. Are These 'School Shootings'?," *Vox*, March 5, 2018, https://www.vox.com/2018/3/5/17036856/school-shootings-gun-violence-america.

6. Sherman, "Do Most Mass Shootings Happen in Gun-Free Zones?"

7. Brian Montopoli, "What Does Jared Lee Loughner Believe?," CBS News, January 10, 2011, https://www.cbsnews.com/news/what-does-jared-lee-loughner-believe/; "Congresswoman Gabrielle Giffords Injured in Shooting Rampage," History, January 8, 2011, https://www.history.com/this-day-in-history/congresswoman-gabrielle-giffords-injured-in-shooting-rampage.

8. John Bowden, "Capitol Hill Police Officer Left Weapon Unattended in Capitol Bathroom," *The Hill*, February 27, 2019, https://thehill.com/blogs/blog-briefing-room/news/431924-capitol-police-officer-left-weapon-unattended-in-capitol/.

9. Robert Ebert, "Elephant," RobertEbert.com, November 7, 2003, https://www.rogerebert.com/reviews/elephant-2003.

10. Matthew Impelli, "Buffalo Shooter Saw New York's Gun Laws as His Advantage," *Newsweek*, May 16, 2022, https://www.newsweek.com/buffalo-shooter-saw-new-yorks-gun-laws-his-advantage-1706982.

11. "Hiram Percy Maxim," in *Encyclopedia Britannica*, August 29, 2022, https://www.britannica.com/biography/Hiram-Percy-Maxim.

12. David R. Henderson, "TANSTAAFL, There Ain't No Such Thing as a Free Lunch," EconLib.org, March 3, 2014, https://www.econlib.org/library/Columns/y2014/Hendersontanstaafl.html.

13. "The Company," SB Tactical, 2022, https://www.sb-tactical.com/about/company/.

14. Courtney Rozen, "Biden Moves to Regulate Pistol Braces to Help Curb Gun Violence," Bloomberg Law, May 18, 2021, https://news.bloomberglaw .com/social-justice/biden-moves-to-regulate-pistol-braces-as-gun-violence -measure.

15. Lee Williams, "FBI Arrest of Florida Man for Short-Barreled Rifle Showcases Absurdity of NFA," Ammoland, July 13, 2022, https://www .ammoland.com/2022/07/fbi-arrest-of-florida-man-for-short-barreled-rifle -showcases-absurdity-of-nfa/#ixzz7Z5U1t47s.

16. "Shoestring Machine Gun," Endo, January 25, 2010, https://www .everydaynodaysoff.com/2010/01/25/shoestring-machine-gun/.

17. Stephanie M. Boucher to Jeffrey E. Folloder, February 24, 2016, https:// www.nfatca.org/pubs/MG_Count_FOIA_2016.pdf.

18. Jacob Sullum, "SCOTUS Vacates 4 Decisions Upholding Gun Control Laws Whose Constitutionality Now Looks Doubtful," *Reason*, July 1, 2022, https://reason.com/2022/07/01/scotus-vacates-4-decisions-upholding -gun-control-laws-whose-constitutionality-now-looks-doubtful/.

19. Associated Press, "Gun Applicants in New York Will Have to Submit Their Social Accounts for Review," NPR, July 8, 2022, https://www.npr.org /2022/07/08/1110477445/gun-applicants-social-media-accounts-new-york.

20. Kristin Wilson and Daniella Diaz, "House Passes 'Red Flag' Bill as Part of Gun Control Push," CNN, June 9, 2022, https://www.cnn.com/2022/06 /09/politics/red-flag-bill-guns/index.html.

21. Eliza Collins, Siobhan Hughes, and Teresa Mettela, "Senate Passes Bipartisan Gun Bill Funding Red-Flag Laws, Mental Health Programs," MSN, June 24, 2022, https://www.msn.com/en-us/news/politics/senate -passes-bipartisan-gun-bill-funding-red-flag-laws-mental-health-programs /ar-AAYMGLV.

22. Awr Hawkins, "House Democrats Moving on 'Assault Weapons' Ban: Targets at Least 45 Specific AR-15 Rifles," Breitbart, July 15, 2022, https:// www.breitbart.com/politics/2022/07/15/house-democrats-moving-on -assault-weapons-ban-targets-at-least-45-specific-ar-15-rifles/.

23. Emily Zanotti, "Harvey Weinstein Hasn't Delivered on His Promise to 'Fight the NRA,'" DailyWire+, October 24, 2017, https://www.dailywire .com/news/harvey-weinstein-hasnt-delivered-his-promise-fight-emily-zanotti.

Chapter Seven

1. Annette Doerr, "Tueller Drill: What Is It? Why Does It Matter?," Guns. com, May 11, 2022, https://www.guns.com/news/tueller-drill.

2. Active Self Protection (channel), YouTube, https://www.youtube.com /c/ActiveSelfProtection/featured.

3. Associated Press, Chris Wolfe, John Fenoglio, Lauren Lyster, and Kareen Wynter, "Bodycam Video Released in Fatal Police Shooting of Black Teen Girl Swinging Knife in Columbus, Ohio," KTLA, April 22, 2021, https:// ktla.com/news/nexstar-media-wire/nationworld/bodycam-video-released -in-fatal-police-shooting-of-black-teen-girl-swinging-knife-in-columbus-ohio/.

Conclusion

1. "Self-Defense for College Students," U.S. Law Shield, March 30, 2022, https://www.uslawshield.com/self-defense-for-college-students/.

2. "A Brief History of the NRA," NRA, 2022, https://home.nra.org/about -the-nra/; David Kopel and Joseph Greenlee, "The Racist Origin of Gun Control Laws," *The Hill*, August 22, 2017, https://thehill.com/blogs /pundits-blog/civil-rights/347324-the-racist-origin-of-gun-control-laws/; Thomas R. Eddlem, "The Racist Origin of America's Gun Control Laws," *New American*, September 9, 2014, https://thenewamerican.com/the-racist -origin-of-america-s-gun-control-laws/.

3. Jonathan Vankin, "California Gun Control: How Ronald Reagan and the Black Panthers Started a Movement," California Local, April 13, 2022, https://californialocal.com/localnews/statewide/ca/article/show/4412 -california-gun-control-reagan-black-panthers/; Thaddeus Morgan, "The NRA Supported Gun Control When the Black Panthers Had the Weapons," History, August 30, 2018, https://www.history.com/news/black-panthers -gun-control-nra-support-mulford-act.

4. Smooth Media, "NFAC Leader Grandmaster Jay Incorrectly Explains Why His Militia Accidentally Shot Themselves," YouTube, August 1, 2020, https://www.youtube.com/watch?v=cgB085H44s0.

5. "VIDEO: NFAC Protester's Negligent Discharge Injures 3 in Louisville," Personal Defense World, December 29, 2021, https://www.personal defenseworld.com/2020/07/nfac-negligent-discharge-louisville/.

6. "NSSF: Record Gun Sales in 2020 Including among Minorities," GunMag. com, February 5, 2021, http://www.thegunmag.com/nssf-record-gun-sales -in-2020-including-among-minorities/; "NICS Firearm Checks: Month/ Year," FBI, 2022, https://www.fbi.gov/file-repository/nics_firearm_checks _-_month_year.pdf/view.

7. Peter Suciu, "Gun Ownership on the Rise among Women and Minorities," *National Interest*, January 10, 2022, https://nationalinterest.org/blog/buzz /gun-ownership-rise-among-women-and-minorities-199275.

8. Ashe Schow, "Women, Minorities Leading Increase in Conceal Carry Permits," DailyWire+, October 7, 2020, https://www.dailywire.com/news /women-minorities-leading-increase-in-conceal-carry-permits.

9. Mensah M. Dean, "As More People Get Guns and Carry Permits Philly Sees a Sharp Rise in Homicides Ruled Justified," *Philadelphia Inquirer*, June 20, 2022, https://www.inquirer.com/news/justified-homicide-self -defense-philadelphia-police-larry-krasner-gun-license-permit-20220620 .html.

10. Awr Hawkins, "Philadelphia: Fatal Self-Defense Shootings Soar as Concealed Carry Applications Rise," Breitbart, June 20, 2022, https://www .breitbart.com/2nd-amendment/2022/06/20/justifiable-homicides-rise -philadelphia-concealed-carry-surges/.

11. "About the Pink Pistols," Pink Pistols, https://www.pinkpistols.org/about -the-pink-pistols/.

Index